UPPER EGYPT

Historical Outline and Descriptive Guide to the Ancient Sites

Jill Kamil

Photographs by Carolyn Brown and Peter Clayton
Plans and maps by Elizabeth Rodenbeck and Hassan Ibrahim

LONGMAN
LONDON AND NEW YORK

Longman Group Limited
Longman House, Burnt Mill, Harlow,
Essex CM20 2JE, England
and Associated companies throughout the world

Longman Inc.,
19 West 44th Street,
New York, NY 10036
© Longman Group Ltd 1983

First published 1983
Second impression 1986
ISBN 0 582 78314 3

British Library Cataloguing in Publication Data
Kamil, Jill
Upper Egypt.
1. Egypt—History—to 640 A.D.
I. Title
932   DT83
ISBN 0-582-78314-3

Library of Congress Cataloging in Publication Data
Kamil, Jill.
Upper Egypt.
Includes index.
1. Egypt—Antiquities—Guide-books
2. Egypt—Description and travel—1945–   —Guide-books.
I. Title
DT60.K28 1983   916.2´0454   82-8949
ISBN 0-582-78314-3 (pbk.)   AACR2

Produced by Longman Group (FE) Ltd
Printed in Hong Kong

For Timothy Bull and Ricos

ACKNOWLEDGMENTS

The author would like to thank Dr Labib Habachi, formerly Director of Field Work of the Antiquities Department and Member of the Institut d'Egypte, for his help and guidance in the preparation of this book, Professor Michael Dols for reading the manuscript, Nadia Haggar for inspiring the work, and Timmy for her valuable suggestions and constant encouragement.

The publishers are indebted to Mr Peter Clayton for his advice and encouragement and for the photographs appearing on pages 33, 125, 157, 164, 173, 198, and the cover subject.

Cover photograph: *Felucca on the Nile*

CONTENTS

Page

PART II

PART III

PLANS AND MAPS

References to the plans and maps:

References in the text to the plans are always in full: (Plan 14) etc.
Italic numbers and letters in brackets refer to points of interest within a particular plan. (*P.1*), (*P.2*), for example, always indicate first pylon, second pylon etc.

PREFACE

This book has been divided into three parts.

PART I   PHARAONIC PERIOD (3100–332 BC)
PART II   GRAECO-ROMAN PERIOD (332 BC–AD 395)
PART III   EARLY CHRISTIAN PERIOD

The sites have been given historical perspective by placing them chronologically. That is to say, the peak period of each site governs its position. This enables the book to serve its main purpose as a practical guide to the monuments, and, at the same time, to be read as history through the historical overlap in the Background to each chapter.

Abydos comes first because it was near here that Narmer (Menes) was born, the first pharaoh, who united the Two Lands of Upper and Lower Egypt (3100 BC). It is followed by **Aswan**, whose powerful noblemen were 'Keepers of the Southern Gate' in the Old Kingdom (2686–2181 BC). **Luxor** rose to importance in the Middle Kingdom (2133–1786 BC) and became capital of the empire in the New Kingdom (1567–1080 BC), with only the short setback of Akhenaten to hinder its growth. **Tel el Amarna** was the site chosen by Akhenaten and occupied for only a short period (1375–1350 BC).

Nubia and **Kush**, Egypt's southern neighbours became completely Egyptianised in the New Kingdom. After a period of decline, the Kushites came to Egypt's rescue and ruled from 750 to 656 BC. They were overthrown by the Assyrians and returned to Kush (Sudan) where they founded their own kingdom. This Meroitic Kingdom later challenged Egypt (181 BC), which was then ruled by the Ptolemies.

Graeco-Roman Egypt is divided into the Ptolemaic period 332–30 BC), when the country developed into the most prosperous and powerful state in the then known world, and when temples like those of **Dendera**, **Esna**, **Edfu**, **Kom Ombo** and **Philae** were built on older foundations; and the Roman period (30 BC–AD 395), when the Egyptians were so hard-pressed to meet the tax requirements imposed by Rome that many sought a life of asceticism. The Graeco-Roman monuments are described from north to south in order that the island of Philae, the last outpost of the Egyptian tradition on its native soil, should immediately precede the Christian Period.

Christianity spread during the Roman period, when a monastic way of life was founded. The concluding chapter points out the remarkable continuity – in location, tradition, ritual and ideology – that persists to the present day.

Naturally the divisions are not perfect. Where Graeco-Roman or early Christian structures are located at predominently Pharaonic sites, however, the reader is referred to the appropriate pages in the Table of Contents and in the text. Moreover, in order to provide comprehensive coverage for each monument, it has been decided to keep each as a descriptive unit, at the expense of some, inevitable, repetition.

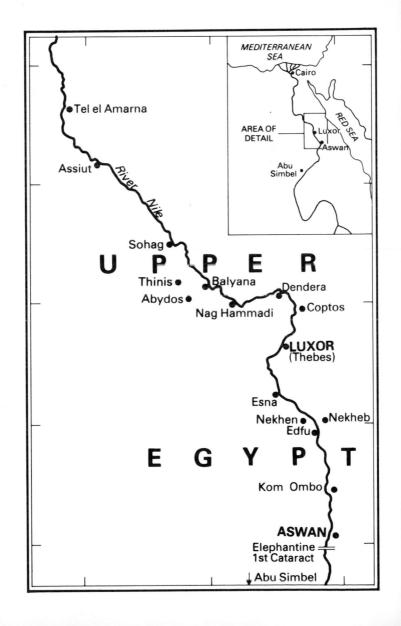

MEDITERRANEAN SEA

Cairo

RED SEA

AREA OF DETAIL

Luxor

Aswan

Abu Simbel

●Tel el Amarna

Assiut●

River Nile

U P P E R

Sohag●

Thinis ●

Balyana●

●Dendera

Abydos ●

●Coptos

Nag Hammadi

●**LUXOR**
(Thebes)

Esna●

E G Y P T

Nekhen ●

●Nekheb

Edfu●

Kom Ombo ●

ASWAN
Elephantine
1st Cataract

↓Abu Simbel

4

NILE VALLEY Plan 1

Buto
Basiris
Abasir Bana

LOWER EGYPT

Heliopolis
Sakkara CAIRO
Memphis

Fayoum

SINAI PENINSULA

RED SEA

Minia
Beni Hassan
Tel el-Amarna

Assiut

R. Nile

U P P E R

Sohag

Balyana
Thinis   Dendera
Abydos   Coptos
Nag Hammadi

Thebes (Luxor)

E G Y P T

Esna
Nekhen   Nekheb
Edfu

Kom Ombo

Elephantine
1st Cataract
↓
Abu Simbel

Aswan

INTRODUCTION

THE ENVIRONMENT

Egypt is a land with well defined boundaries. To the east and west are vast deserts. To the north is the Mediterranean Sea. To the south there was a formidable granite barrier – now inundated – beyond which lay the barren land of Nubia.

These physical barriers were, of course, open to cultural influences, and could be traversed by groups of traders. But they impeded large bodies of troops. This gave the ancient Egyptians a great sense of security and confidence. They had the feeling that divine providence protected their land and set them apart from their neighbours. They were the *remeth*, 'the (true) men'. The others were 'sand-dwellers', 'sand-wanderers', or people other than Egyptians. Theirs was a flat and largely uniform landscape, blessed with eternal sunshine and a lifegiving annual flood. Hill country was foreign land

Farmers winnowing grain: Osiris was the 'grain god'

Within these recognisable boundaries, however, was a land divided: Upper Egypt, which extended from Aswan to a point just south of modern Cairo, was, apart from the narrow strip of land flanking the river, largely barren. The triangle of the Delta, or Lower Egypt, was extremely fertile. The climate in Upper Egypt was semi-tropical. That of the Delta was temperate. Such physical and climatic differences naturally gave rise to different cultures, different experiences and different outlooks.

Black-topped pottery of Upper Egypt

Wavy-handled, buff coloured jars from Lower Egypt

Pre-dynastic pottery, for example, was stamped, like the land itself, by a distinct character; black-topped, burnished ware was found in Upper Egypt, and wide-lipped, buff-coloured pottery in Lower Egypt. The inhabitants of Upper Egypt remained semi-nomadic even after those of Lower Egypt had settled down to farming. Control of river water in largely barren Upper Egypt required the digging of canals and blockage in basins against times of need. In the Delta settlements were made on natural knolls. The hardy Upper Egyptians, who were closely linked with Nubia and Kush, tended to be somewhat suspicious by nature. The Lower Egyptians, culturally oriented to the Mediterranean and the lands of Asia, were tolerant of strangers.

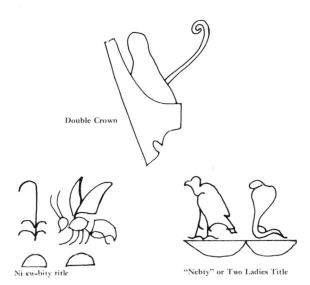

Double Crown

Ni-sw-bity title

"Nebty" or Two Ladies Title

These two titles appear beside the oblong *cartouche* bearing the pharaoh's name in temple reliefs. The first combines the ancient symbols of Upper and Lower Egypt, the sedge-plant and the bee; the second is a combination of the vulture-goddess Nekheb in Upper Egypt and the cobra-goddess of Buto in Lower Egypt. The titles mean unity between the Two Lands, as does the 'Double Crown', combining the White Crown and the Red Crown.

Little wonder, then, that dualism should enter into the very political organisation of the country, which was reflected in the Two Lands of Upper and Lower Egypt. The ruler was Lord of the Two Lands, even at a time when the frontiers of Egypt were extended well beyond its borders.

Unification has been ascribed to Narmer (Menes). He was the first king to be portrayed wearing both the White Crown of Upper Egypt and the Red Crown of Lower Egypt, having brought the whole of the Nile valley under his domination from the First Cataract, south of Aswan, to the Mediterranean sea.

Social attitudes, however, did not end with unification. In fact they remained such that an Egyptian exile, bewildered at finding himself in a foreign country, wrote that '. . .*it was as if a man of the Delta were to see himself in Elephantine.*' And the different dialects of the people of Upper and Lower Egypt were expressed thus: '. . . *your speeches . . . are confused when heard . . . they are like the words of a man of the Delta marshes with a man of Elephantine.*'

(Erman, A. *The Literature of the Ancient Egyptian.* Eng. translation A.M. Blackman, London 1927)

HISTORICAL OUTLINE

We owe the division of Egypt's ancient history into thirty royal Dynasties from Menes to Alexander the Great to an Egyptian historian called Manetho, who lived in the reign of Ptolemy II (285–247 BC). The Dynasties were subsequently combined and grouped into three main periods: the Old Kingdom or Pyramid Age, the Middle Kingdom, and the New Kingdom. These have been further divided by modern historians into:

Early Dynastic Period	3100–2686 BC
1st Dynasty	
2nd Dynasty	
Old Kingdom	2686–2181 BC
3rd Dynasty	
4th Dynasty	
5th Dynasty	
6th Dynasty	
First Intermediate Period	2181–2133 BC
7th/8th Dynasties	
9th to early 11th Dynasties	
Middle Kingdom	2133–1786 BC
11th Dynasty	
12th Dynasty	
Second Intermediate Period	1786–1567 BC
13th to 17th Dynasties	
New Kingdom	1567–1080 BC
18th Dynasty	
19th Dynasty	
20th Dynasty	
Third Intermediate Period (Period of Decline)	1080–715 BC
21st to 24th Dynasties	

Late Period

25th Dynasty (Kushite)	**750–656** BC
26th Dynasty (Saite)	**664–525** BC
27th to 30th Dynasties	
(mostly Persian)	**525–332** BC

It is perhaps not surprising, in view of the more hostile environment in Upper Egypt and the economic attraction of the fertile Delta, that the thrust towards unification was always spearheaded from Upper Egypt.

Menes came from ancient Thinis, near Abydos, and according to Manetho the first and second Dynasties were ruled by 'eight kings of Thinis' and 'nine kings of Thinis' respectively. This was a period in which there appears to have been active resistance against unity. Once consolidated, however, Egypt embarked on a period of economic prosperity, technical achievement, productivity and inventiveness. During the Old Kingdom (2686–2345 BC) a series of vigorous monarchs established and maintained a highly centralised government. This was when the pharaohs Khufu (Cheops), Khafre (Chephren) and Menkaure (Mycerinus) raised the great pyramids on the Giza plateau.

Unfortunately, forces of internal erosion finally reduced the country to lawlessness, and the monarchy fell. The provincial lords who had gained prestige under the great pharaohs agitated for independence. The country fragmented into small provincial kingdoms, and though several leaders governed independently during the First Intermediate Period, none was powerful enough to rule the Two Lands.

It was an Upper Egyptian from the Theban area, Luxor, who provided the stimulus to reunify the country and pave the way for the Middle Kingdom (2133–1786 BC), the second cultural peak. Four pharaohs by the name of Amenemhet and three called Senusert (Sesostris) ruled during the 12th Dynasty, a period of great prosperity. It was comparable to, but in many ways different from, the Old Kingdom. Fine monuments were raised throughout the land; arts and crafts again flourished, and irrigation projects were carried out. Furthermore, Egypt extended its frontiers well into Kush, where a series of enormous frontier fortresses were established.

As before, there was a breakdown in the central government. Petty kings ruled simultaneously from Luxor in Upper Egypt and from some centres in Lower Egypt. Rapid decline set in and the country soon passed under the domination of the Hyksos, 'rulers of foreign countries', warlike tribes from western Asia.

The Hyksos occupation lasted for about a century. Again it was a family from Thebes who triggered the war of liberation and provided the galvanic response to pursue the enemy right into their own camp, which was situated in the north-eastern Delta. Having successfully defeated the enemy and driven them out of Egypt, a liberated, reunited country could embark on its third cultural peak.

Under the rulers of the New Kingdom (1567–1080 BC), Egypt developed into an important power. The successful wars against the Hyksos had already transformed the country into a military state with a standing army. Now it remained to create an empire and extend the frontiers southwards to Kush and north-eastwards to the countries of Palestine and Syria. The monuments raised throughout the land during the New Kingdom, particularly those in Upper Egypt, reflect the wealth and prosperity of the nation. Unfortunately, the pharaohs fell under the domination of the high priests of Amon at Thebes, until eventually one of them seized the throne.

In the 21st Dynasty, the country was once more divided: Upper Egypt was ruled by the high priests at Thebes, and Lower Egypt by a family in Tanis. Under a divided and weakened rule, Egypt succumbed again to foreign invasion: tribes of Libyan origin, Kushites from beyond Nubia, the Assyrian conquest and then, following a short-lived revival known as the Saite Period, came the Persian invasions, and finally the Greek and Roman occupations.

White Crown

Red Crown

In times of strong central government, the Two Lands of Upper and Lower Egypt were united. In times of weakened rule they broke apart. When united, the culture was built on strong foundations of inherited values and traditions. When divided, the Delta, Lower Egypt, was open to diverse foreign influences, while it was in Upper Egypt, and in neighbouring Nubia, that the traditional spirit of ancient Egypt survived.

12

ABYDOS (NORTHERN SITES) Plan 2

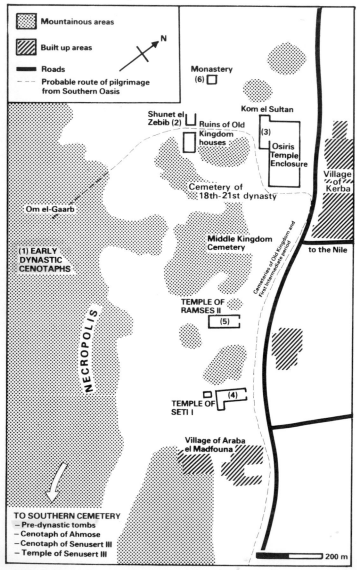

PART I

PHARAONIC PERIOD (3100–332 BC)

CHAPTER 1   ABYDOS

BACKGROUND

Abydos (the Greek version of the ancient Egyptian name *Abdu*) is situated on the western bank of the Nile about seven kilometres west of the modern town of Balyana. It made its debut on the stage of Egypt's ancient history even before the Dynastic period and retained its aura of sanctity longer than any other site in Egypt. This was because <u>Abydos was the cult centre of Osiris</u>, Egypt's most beloved hero and the central figure of the country's most popular myth.

The Osiris Myth

The **Osiris myth** is one of the most poignant, and probably the most well-known of ancient Egypt. Surviving in oral tradition and variably recounted over the centuries, it has come down to us in many versions and with many contradictions. The earliest Egyptian sources are the Pyramid Texts (*c.* 2345–2181 BC), where the story is not in connected form. The most complete version is given by Plutarch, the Greek writer (*c.* 46–*c.* 126 AD).

According to the earliest version of the myth, Osiris, with his devoted wife Isis at his side, was a just god who ruled wisely and well. His brother Set, however, was jealous of his popularity and secretly sought to do away with him. At a rural festival Set enticed his visitors to try out a marvellously fashioned chest for size. When it came to Osiris' turn, he unsuspectingly obliged, unaware that it had been made to his exact measurements. As soon as he lay down in it Set and his accomplices fell on the chest, shut the lid, and cast it into the Nile to be carried away by the flood.

Isis was overwhelmed with grief at the news. She cast sand on her hair, rent her robes in sorrow, and set out in search of the chest. When she finally found it, she hid it beneath a tamarisk tree. Unfortunately, Set was out hunting and came upon the hiding place. He extracted the body, which he brutally tore into fourteen pieces, scattering them far and wide.

The tormented Isis, this time in the company of her sister, the goddess Nephthys, set out once more on a harrowing journey to collect the pieces of the body. Having done so, she and Nephthys called on the gods to help them bind the parts together and restore the body to life. Isis crooned incantations until breath came to the nostrils of Osiris, sight to his eyes and movement to his limbs. Then, the devoted wife, in the form of a bird, descended on Osiris and received his seed. When Isis gave birth to her son, Horus, she nursed him in solitude, and raised him to manhood to avenge his father's death.

The tales of Isis' devotion to her son Horus are many and varied. She brought him up secretly in the marshes of the Delta until he was strong. Then Horus set out in search of Set, his father's slayer, and many and terrible were the battles between them. Horus, however, triumphed over evil, and emerged as victor. With the approval of the gods the throne was restored to him.

The Pyramid Texts are full of references to the faithful wife seeking the body of her husband. The weeping and lamentations of Isis and Nephthys for Osiris were a widespread and sacred expression of sorrow to the Egyptians. They loved to dwell on the loyalty and devotion of Isis, the evil of Set and the filial piety of Horus. They rewove the tale in their many oral renditions and dramatized them in public performances. (For later versions of the myth see pages 184 and 186.)

The Legendary Ancestor

It is thought that Osiris may have been an actual leader in pre-history who was loved and respected by the community. Since his name is associated with the Nile – as a source of fertility – and with the death and rebirth of the land, he may have led his people to an understanding of the benefits of water control and crop rotation at a time when organized farming was first being introduced. When Osiris was killed by critical and jealous opponents, the sorrowing community who had followed him as a just and enlightened leader honoured him in death, when a form of ancestor-worship developed.

It is not known where Osiris ruled. The most prevalent and widely accepted belief is that is was in the province of *Djedu* (near Abusir Bana) in the middle of the Delta, where the district was named after him: *Per-Usire*, or House of Osiris, which was rendered into Busiris by the Greeks. However, the earliest rulers of which we have historical evidence came from Thinis, neighbouring Abydos, and Osiris, the deified ancestor, came to have a prominent place there from early times, overshadowing Wepwawat, the wolf-jackal, the first god of the area.

The Thinite leaders slowly spread their influence. They moved southwards as far as Nekhen (Gr. Hierakonpolis), near the modern town of Edfu, which became the pre-dynastic capital of Upper Egypt, and northwards towards the Delta. A large macehead excavated at Nekhen records a military victory of an Upper Egyptian king (known as the "Scorpion King") over the chieftains of the Delta (symbolically depicted as dead birds hung from Upper Egyptian standards). The main theme of this macehead is agricultural; the central register shows the king wielding a hoe in both hands and breaking ground amidst scenes of rejoicing.

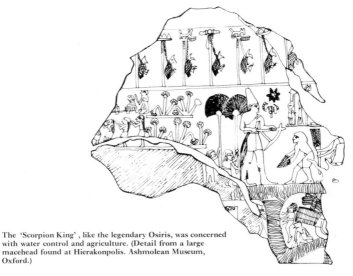

The 'Scorpion King', like the legendary Osiris, was concerned with water control and agriculture. (Detail from a large macehead found at Hierakonpolis. Ashmolean Museum, Oxford.)

Unification of the Two Lands has been attributed to Narmer (Menes) who was also a native of Thinis. He was the first pharaoh to be shown wearing the Red Crown of Lower Egypt in addition to the White Crown of Upper Egypt. According to tradition, when he chose Memphis – a site near the border between the Two Lands – as capital, he diverted the river in order to render it more suitable for habitation. Therefore, although the palette symbolically depicted his triumph over the Delta on one side, and unification on the other, Narmer, too, was traditionally associated with water control.

The Palette of Narmer, also excavated from Nekhen (Hierakonopolis) in Upper Egypt, shows the Pharaoh Narmer wearing the White Crown on one side, and the Red Crown on the other. (Cairo Museum.)

Narmer and his successors of the 1st and 2nd Dynasties (3100–2686 BC) ruled from Memphis (then known as the 'White Wall'), and were buried in huge funerary monuments on the necropolis of Memphis (Sakkara). Nevertheless, they honoured their ancestral home. Among the barren hills west of Abydos they constructed impressive cenotaphs (1), where relatives and friends could make suitable offerings.

With the passage of time, the legendary ancestor Osiris, and the half-forgotten kings of Thinis of the first two Dynasties, became associated in the minds of the people. The Nile valley dwellers, who traditionally honoured the graves of their forefathers, came to pay homage at the cenotaphs on the necropolis of Abydos in the conviction that Osiris was buried there.

The ruins of the cenotaph of Hor Aha (who has been identified with Narmer, the first pharaoh of recorded history), show that it was brick-lined, and the underground chamber measured 12 × 9 metres. His successor, Djer, had an even larger structure of some 21 × 20 metres. It was the latter cenotaph, of Djer, that came to be regarded by the ancient Egyptians as the burial place of Osiris.

The central chamber of Djer's cenotaph was surrounded on three sides by irregular chambers, and there is indication that the whole structure was originally roofed with wooden beams. Surrounding it were no less than 338 subsidiary graves, many with crude stone stelae recording the names of the deceased who died after the pharaoh. It is possible that they may have believed that to be buried near the tomb or cenotaph of their master would ensure them a happy afterlife themselves.

During the Old Kingdom (2686–2181 BC) the centre of activity was at Memphis and Giza. But the great pharaohs did not neglect Abydos. Decrees were promulgated to safeguard the interests of the priests of sacred sites. There were endowments for meat and milk to be placed at the holy places on official feast days. There is evidence, too, that some of the pharaohs travelled to Abydos. Whether this was part of their official duties or a pilgrimage is not known. There is a rectangular enclosure of crenellated brick, known as Shunet el Zebib (2) that is thought to date to the early Dynasties; and worth mentioning is that the only statue ever found of the pharaoh Khufu (builder of the Great Pyramid of Giza) is a tiny ivory statuette excavated from the area of Abydos.

By the end of the 5th Dynasty (2345 BC) the name of Osiris had crept into the mortuary literature as an explicit example of rebirth; the deceased was referred to as 'Osiris', meaning deceased and reborn 'like Osiris'. The earliest shrine at Abydos, however, was not in honour of Osiris but of Wepwawat, the wolf-jackal of the necropolis, whose function was to protect the dead from prowling animals at the edge of the desert. It was built by the 6th Dynasty pharaoh Pepi I at a site now known as Kom el Sultan (3).

Cult Centre at Abydos

During the Middle Kingdom (2133–1786 BC) Abydos was fully established as a city of prime importance and a place of pilgrimage. The 12th Dynasty pharaoh Senusert I erected a large edifice on the site of the earlier shrine at Kom el Sultan, which became known as the Temple of Osiris. Senusert III completely renovated it during his reign, and surrounded it with an enclosure wall. Influential noblemen were permitted to place stelae or erect cenotaphs near the sacred area. For it had become desirable to have a monument constructed at or near Abydos, in order for the spirit of the deceased to join in the annual dramatization of the life, death and triumph of Osiris, enacted by the priests.

Each year, settlers would come from far and wide to see the ritualistic killing of Osiris by his brother Set, followed by several days of mourning. The people would show appropriate sorrow for the murdered god and weep and lament in the manner of Isis. Funerary wreaths and flowers would be placed on a mummified figure of Osiris that was borne through the city. The cortège would

Erecting the *Djed* pillar, symbol of Osiris. Seti temple, Abydos

be led by Wepwawat, the wolf-jackal, 'He who opens the way'. The people would sing hymns and make offerings, and at a prescribed site a mock battle would take place between Horus and Set. The murder of Osiris was avenged, and the triumphant procession returned to the temple. The crowning scene was the erection of the backbone of Osiris, the *Djed* or pillar-like fetish. In horizontal position the *Djed* represented the slain hero and the low Nile. Upright it symbolised the resurrection of Osiris, as well as the flood and the rebirth of the land.

One of the functions of mythology was to explain certain natural, social or political ideas. The mythical Osiris (who was associated with the rebirth of the land) falling victim to Set (who was associated with the relentless desert) explained the physical environment; the constant battle against the encroaching desert. Set's tearing the body of Osiris to pieces and scattering its parts up and down the Nile valley may be interpreted as the concept of sowing grain, following which, with the necessary incantations (like those performed by Isis and Nephthys), or rural festivals, the stalks of grain would be reborn (as Osiris was reborn). Horus, the son of the gods related to the rebirth of the land, triumphed over the desert (Set) and became prototype of the pharaohs.

In the Middle Kingdom the ordinary man could aspire to do what only members of the aristocracy had done before: pay homage to the legendary ancestor. Thousands of pilgrims from all walks of life made their way to the necropolis where Osiris was worshipped as 'Osiris Khenti-Amentiu', an epithet that means 'he who rules the west'. Generation's after generation's offerings in pottery vessels were left at the cenotaph of Djer, which was believed to be the tomb of Osiris. Today the site has acquired the name of *Om el Gaab* ('mother of potsherds').

To identify with the resurrected deity, it had long become common practice to place grain in a mummy-shaped linen container, water it and let it germinate through the cloth. This so-called 'Body of Osiris' was an example of his power to give life. It was believed that the mummy, like the grain, would revive.

The cult of Osiris had thoroughly captured the popular imagination. The provincial priests who wished to give importance to their areas each claimed that a part of the body, dismembered by Set, was buried in their province. In one variation of the myth the head was said to be buried at Abydos. In another version it was the whole body that had been found there with the exception of the phallus that had been eaten by an Oxyrynchos fish. *Abdu*, Abydos, had by this time become the centre of the cult. It means 'the mound of the Osiris head emblem'.

During the New Kingdom (1567–1080 BC), Abydos rose to its peak as a holy city. This was the empire period, when the state could afford to be generous. Thutmose I ordered a barge of cedar and electrum to be built for Osiris, and almost every pharaoh of the 18th Dynasty left evidence of his devotion to the god, making additions to the temple at Kom el Sultan. Thutmose III, in particular, carried out new work and restoration; and Thutmose IV arranged for the regular supply of sacrificial animals and birds for feasts and festivals.

Deceased noblemen from Thebes, the capital, were often borne, after embalming, to Abydos and placed in the precinct of the temple. Afterwards they were returned and interred at Thebes. If they could not make the pilgrimage, it was made symbolically; many tomb reliefs show boats bearing the deceased to Abydos (page 105f).

In the 19th Dynasty, Abydos and its chief deity were honoured by Seti I on an unprecedented scale. He raised the three gods of the Osirian Triad (Osiris, Isis and Horus) to an even higher level than the greatest gods of the land (Ptah of Memphis, Amon-Ra of Thebes, and Ra-Harakhte of Heliopolis). He constructed a marvellous temple (4), with separate sanctuaries for each deity and with a seventh chamber, of equal size, to himself as a god (page 26). His son

Seti I shows his son, Ramses II, the list of royal ancestors. Seti temple, Abydos

and successor, Ramses II, built a temple of his own (5) to the north (page 29).

The decline of the cult of Osiris only came in the Graeco-Roman period (Part II, Ch. 6), when the seat of Osiris worship was shifted to Bigeh Island, and that of Isis to Philae. This might well have been done in an attempt to break the power of the wealthy and influential priesthood at Abydos. Thenceforth the cult of Isis outrivalled that of Osiris. Philae became the most holy place in Egypt and the centre of the most popular cult (page 183).

During the Graeco-Roman period, Abydos came to be regarded as a place of healing. Sufferers from all over the Graeco-Roman world gathered in the corridors and halls of the temple of Seti I, making humble pleas for health or fertility. The graffiti are in hieratic (a late development of hieroglyphics), Greek, Phoenician and Aramaic.

When Christianity spread to Upper Egypt, Seti's temple was used by the early Christians escaping from Roman persecution. Later two ancient structures were used as convents, and the Monastery of St Moses was built to the north (6). (Chapter 8, page 204.)

DESCRIPTION OF MONUMENTS

General
The monuments that are most frequently visited at Abydos are the New Kingdom temples of Seti I and Ramses II, and not those for which the ancient city was famous. The cenotaphs of the 1st and 2nd Dynasties are no more than ruins. Of the great temple of Osiris at Kom el Sultan, only the granite doorways and paving stones remain. The many cemeteries of different periods are not tourist sites. The temple of Seti I, however, makes a visit to Abydos well worthwhile because it is decorated with some of the finest relief sculpture of any age to be found in the Nile valley. Moreover, the reliefs of the nearby temple of Ramses II are so finely carved that they lead us to suspect that the temple was constructed at the beginning of his reign, and decorated by the very artists who worked under his father, Seti I.

Seti I bows slightly to the enthroned Horus. Seti temple, Abydos

Temple of Seti I
Seti I was the son of an army officer. In fact, he himself commanded the frontier garrison at what is known as Kantara in the eastern Delta. When he came to the throne in 1318 BC, he proved to be one of Egypt's most able pharaohs, known particularly for encouraging an artistic and architectural revival. Seti I seems to have desired a

return to the orthodox canons of Egyptian art after the breakaway
art movement in the 'Amarna period' (page 118). The representations in his temple are majestic, delicate and conservative; they
also have an additional quality reminiscent of the naturalism of the
Amarna period; emotional expression. Although the many representations of Seti appear to be alike, on close scrutiny they will be
seen to be slightly different from one another. As he looks into the
face of an honoured deity, for example, his expression is one of
reverence. Before a goddess, there is a look of loving trust. Before
one of the great gods, he bends slightly at the waist to indicate awe.
This latter pose is not to be found in any representations of the 18th
Dynasty, where the pharaoh always stood proudly erect and exalted.
The gods, too, are depicted with human emotions. Osiris looks
benevolent and majestic. Isis is gracious and tender. Horus is
competent and direct.

Seti I in sacred barge, with a goddess

The temple of Seti I is built of fine-textured limestone and has
many unique features: one is a wing at the southwest corner
(compare with traditional temple page 63), another is the so-called
Osirion (page 28), and, most unusual, is the seven-fold dedication.
The temple of Seti has sanctuaries for Osiris, Isis and Horus (the
Triad associated with Abydos), Ptah the god of Memphis (the first

capital of a united country), Ra-Harakhte (the Sun-god of Heliopolis), Amon-Ra (the 'King of Gods' and God of Thebes) and the last shrine for Seti himself.

The **Entrance Pylon** and **First Court** (1) are in ruin. Only the rear section of the Second Court (2) is preserved. It is approached by a graded stairway leading to a terrace on which there were twelve square pillars; on each pillar Ramses II, son of Seti I, is depicted embracing the principal gods of Egypt. The text on the walls to the rear relate, at (a), that when Ramses came to Abydos and found that the temple of his father was unfinished and neglected he completed it for him. To the left of the central doorway (b) is a large representation of Ramses offering the symbol of Truth to Osiris, Isis and to his late father Seti I.

To the right of the doorway (c) there are representations of Horus, Isis and Seti I, following which, at (d), Ramses II is shown beside the sacred tree of Heliopolis. Ptah, god of Memphis, writes his name on the leaves. Thoth, the god of Wisdom, records the event. Ra-Harakhte presents Ramses with the royal crook and flail. Behind Ra-Harakhte, Osiris is depicted.

The first **Hypostyle Hall** (3) is 60 metres wide and about 14 metres deep. It is roofed and supported by 24 papyrus-bud columns arranged in pairs. The hall was originally designed to be entered through seven doorways, which led to another seven doorways, and ultimately to the appropriate shrine of each of the seven deities. All but two were, however, blocked by Ramses II.

The decoration of this hall was also carried out by Ramses II. He is shown making offerings to, or obtaining blessings from, the various gods and goddesses. Noteworthy are the scenes showing his active participation in planning the temple. At (e) he is depicted facing the goddess Seshat, patron deity of records and archives; the goddess is driving stakes into the ground to measure out the ground-plan. Behind Seshat is Osiris, who watches over the activities being conducted on his behalf. Above this scene Ramses breaks ground with a hoe before Osiris. Further along, at (f), Ramses, assisted by Horus, stretches out a measuring rope.

Also noteworthy are the scenes showing temple rituals. All those entering a holy shrine, even royal personages, had to be barefooted and ceremonially pure. Certain acts of ablution were supervised by the priests. This rite is depicted to the left of the entrance doorway (g) where Seti is purified by Amon-Ra of Thebes, and Atum, ancient sun-god of Heliopolis. They pour the emblems symbolising Life and Prosperity over Seti from golden vessels. Near the left-

24

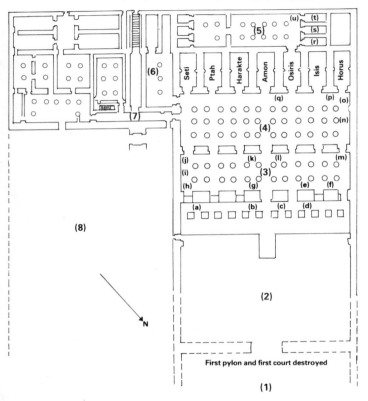

hand corner (h) Seti is purified with water by Thoth and Horus. He is being suckled by Hathor the cow-goddess (i), and is presented to Ptah by Khnum the ram-headed god (j).

To the left of the doorway leading to the Second Hypostyle Hall, at (k), Ramses makes an offering to Amon-Ra and Mut, his consort. To the right (l) he offers them statuettes and burns incense before them. In the corner (m) he presents to Osiris, as owner of the temple, the title deeds that have been written on papyrus, rolled up and placed in an ornamental container.

The **Second Hypostyle Hall** (4) is divided into a front section that is supported by twenty-four sandstone papyrus-bud columns in pairs, and a platform to the rear; the latter forms the threshold to the seven sanctuaries.

Turning to the right-hand wall (n) we find Seti in one scene offering incense and water to Osiris, whose son Horus stands behind him. In the second scene Seti I is shown before a shrine in which Osiris is enthroned (o). This is one of the finest reliefs to be found in the Nile valley. Standing before him are Maat, goddess of Truth and Justice; Renpet, goddess of the year; Isis, who gently supports his arm; Amentet, a goddess of the dead; and Nephthys, sister of Isis.

The **seven shrines**, from right to left, belong to Horus, Isis, Osiris, Amon-Ra, Ra-Harakhte, Ptah and the deified Seti I. The walls between the doorways have niches for offerings. The chambers are decorated with reliefs of Seti making offerings to the appropriate god or to a member of his family. Each shrine has a vaulted roof decorated with stars, flying vultures and Seti's name in oval cartouches. To the rear of each shrine, apart from that of Osiris that leads to the Hall of Osiris in the rear, is a representation of a false doorway, a freize of cobras and a place for a model boat in which the gods themselves made pilgrimages. On feast days these boats would be carried in procession, supported on poles resting on the shoulders of priests.

The representations in the seven shrines depict daily ceremonies performed in each, including the burning of incense, perfuming and anointing the statue of the god, and adorning it with crown and jewels.

In the **Shrine of Horus**, for example, Seti is depicted entering the shrine bearing an incense burner and a libation vase. He opens the doors of the shrine and the various scenes show him offering water and incense to Horus, placing the Double Crown of Upper and Lower Egypt upon his head, adorning him with a necklace (known as the *menat*), the *usekh* collar, and strips of linen that symbolise clothing. Having completed these gestures, Seti leaves the shrine, sweeping the floor behind him in order to remove his footprints.

Similar scenes may be found in the shrines of Isis, Osiris (where some of the figures were damaged by early Christians) and Amon-Ra. All the reliefs are in beautifully preserved colour. In the latter shrine Amon-Ra is depicted in mummified human form and is painted blue. He wears a flat-topped crown and two tall plumes. He is also depicted as Kamutef in ithyphallic form. In another representation the boat of Amon-Ra is shown, with smaller boats for his wife Mut and son Khonsu. The shrines dedicated to Ra-Harakhte and Ptah have similar scenes, but the last shrine, that of Seti, is different from the others.

Shrine of Seti I: Instead of representations of Seti honouring different deities, who, in turn grant him life and prosperity, a priest, representing the god Horus, addresses the nine gods of the Ennead of Heliopolis – Atum-Ra (the Sun-god), Geb (earth) Nut (sky), Shu (air), Tefnut (moisture), Osiris and Isis, Set and Nepthys – on behalf of Seti. We find the goddess Seshat, patron of writing, recording Seti's name and titles. Seti is depicted seated between the goddesses Nekhbet and Wadjet (the vulture and the cobra) that represent Upper and Lower Egypt. Thoth, the god of Wisdom, and Horus, bind together the lotus and the papyrus in a gesture that represents the unity of the Two Lands, beneath the king's name. A priest recites the list of offerings that should be presented to the soul of the deceased.

Seti is also shown seated before a table of offerings, with Thoth reciting the offering list. Above him is his royal barge. The three figures beneath the boat are statues of Seti himself, his father, Ramses I, and Queen Sat-Ra, his mother. A scene from Seti's jubilee shows him seated on a throne borne aloft by three hawk-headed and three jackal-headed figures representing the ancient capitals of Egypt.

Between the shrines are façades in marvellously preserved colour. That between the shrines of Horus and Isis (p) shows Seti receiving the emblems of Upper and Lower Egypt from Horus, and the symbol for a Long Reign from Isis. Below he is embraced by Horus, and receives the symbol of Life from Isis. The façade between the shrines of Osiris and Amon-Ra (q) shows Seti, in the lower scene, seated like a child on the lap of Isis, who caresses him and refers to him as her son. To the left he is embraced by Khonsu, son of Amon-Ra, who holds symbols Life and Prosperity to his face.

The **Hall of Osiris** (5) (approached from the Shrine of Osiris). This hall is twelve metres long and ten metres wide with its roof supported by ten columns. Though it was used by the early Christians, and the hands and faces of the figures were destroyed, the reliefs still retain their original colour. The three small shrines to the right are dedicated to Isis, Seti in Osiris form (i.e. deceased) and Horus.

In the shrine of Horus (r) Seti washes a golden offering table with his hands while Horus extends the emblems of Life, Stability and

Long Reign to him. The inscription proudly records 'Washing the offering-table by the king himself', while Horus declares 'I give you years like those of the Sun-god Ra.' Seti presents incense and libation water to Osiris and Isis. Horus throws a stream of incense into the hot brazier.

In the shrine of Osiris (s), Seti (here identified with Osiris) has holy water poured over him by Horus. The water comes in three streams from triple vases of gold; one stream is in the form of the emblems of Life and Prosperity. Thoth, the god of wisdom, presents the symbol for Life to Osiris and also holds the symbols for each of the Two Lands. Finally, Seti is depicted in the robes of a funerary priest reciting prayers for the dead.

In the shrine of Isis (t) the gentle Isis is shown embracing, protecting and honouring Osiris, Seti, and her son Horus in turn. She stands behind Osiris, holding him with her left arm, and according to the text, she says: 'My two arms are behind thee; I embrace thy beauty.' Then, Seti offers her water and incense and a tray of offerings of bread and fruit, meat and poultry.

On the rear wall (u) of the main hall, Seti I anoints the standard of Abydos while Isis caresses it. To the left is the *Djed* pillar which is ceremoniously raised and placed on its base, symbolising resurrection. Seti offers it strips of linen, in the manner of the adornment of the gods in the various shrines. Then, he lowers it and hands it to Isis for safekeeping.

The Southern Wing of the Temple is composed of a Hall of Sokar (6) and the famous Corridor of Kings (7). Also, there is a western corridor started by Seti but completed by Ramses II; a Hall of Boats where the sacred barges were stored on stone benches along the walls; a court for the slaughter of sacrificial animals; and other chambers for administrative and storage purposes.

The Corridor of Kings contains the famous 'List of Kings' beginning with Narmer and containing seventy-six names in oblong *cartouches*. This important historical record, apart from some notable chronological discrepancies, provides the list of Seti's royal ancestors. The scenes in this corridor give prominence to the young prince Ramses, who was later to reign as Ramses II. He is shown four times as a child helping his father, Seti I, in various religious ceremonies and reading from a papyrus.

Recent excavations have been carried out in the rectangle formed by the main temple and the wing (8). A complex of mud-brick structures was cleared, revealing a large number of store-rooms and also a palace with enthronement hall where Seti received ablutions and observed the progress being made on the building of his temple.

Osirion

This separate structure lies behind the temple of Seti I, to the south-west. Its purpose is unclear and its architectural features are unique. It has variously been called a cenotaph, though it bears no resemblance to such a funerary structure, and a mortuary temple, though there is no other like it. In fact no other structure was surrounded by water.

THE OSIRION Plan 4

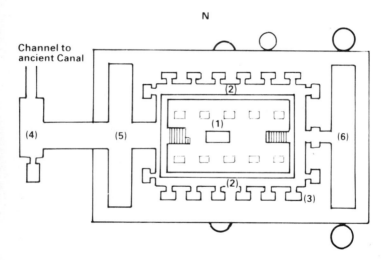

The Osirion is sunk into a depression on a level with the water table. The central hall (1) is surrounded by ditches (2) around which are seventeen rock-hewn niches (3); in front of each was a ledge. The central hall is approached from east and west down a narrow flight of stairs, then led up from the channel of water to the 'island' at the centre. The main part of the structure was built by Seti I, and it was completed by Merenptah, son of Ramses II.

The ante-chamber (4) is decorated with scenes from the mortuary literature, relating to the journey through the under-world (page 87). The transverse chamber to the east (5) is also decorated with scenes from the mortuary literature; that to the west (6) has an arched ceiling and some badly damaged scenes of the cosmogony, featuring the sky-goddess Nut, the earth-god Geb, and Shu the god of the atmosphere.

There seems to have been a long-standing tradition of the sanctity of the area around the Osirion. The 13th Dynasty Pharaoh Neferhotep (*c*. 1786 BC) erected a boundary stele at Abydos; it states that none should set foot there. Such a lingering tradition may have been the reason for Seti choosing to build his temple there. Even today the waters of the Osirion are regarded as advantageous to health. This recalls to mind the hundreds of texts connecting Osiris with Abydos, Osiris with water, and Osiris with rebirth, in which this most beloved figure of ancient Egyptian tradition 'sleeps in the midst of water.'

Temple of Ramses II

This temple is by no means the largest of the temples built by Ramses II, nor is it well preserved; in fact some of the blocks were removed from the monument and reused during the last century. Only the lower part of the walls and the bases of the columns remain. Nevertheless, it will be briefly described because it must once have been among the most beautiful temples in the Nile valley. It was built of fine-grained white limestone, black granite, rose granite, red and brown sandstone, and flawless alabaster. The granite was used for the doorways, sandstone for the columns and alabaster lined the inner shrine.

The **Entrance Pylon** and the **First Court** have, unfortunately, been destroyed. The Second Court (1) is surrounded by a colonnade supported by rectangular pillars; before each was a statue of Ramses in Osiride form. The raised section to the rear (2) was approached by three flights of steps. Its roof was supported by sixteen rectangular sandstone pillars. The highly polished black granite doorway at the centre led to the first Hypostyle Hall (3) and the second Hypostyle Hall (4), one behind the other and both the same size; each contained eight rectangular pillars supporting the roof. There are three shrines on each side of the second Hypostyle Hall. It is not certain to whom they were dedicated.

The door to the rear led to the Sanctuary (5). The roof was constructed of red granite, the upper part of the walls of alabaster, and the lower part of red sandstone. This must undoubtedly have been the most beautiful Sanctuary built in Egypt. The rear wall is an imitation door built of a huge slab of alabaster, which rests on a

30

THE TEMPLE OF RAMSES II AT ABYDOS Plan 5

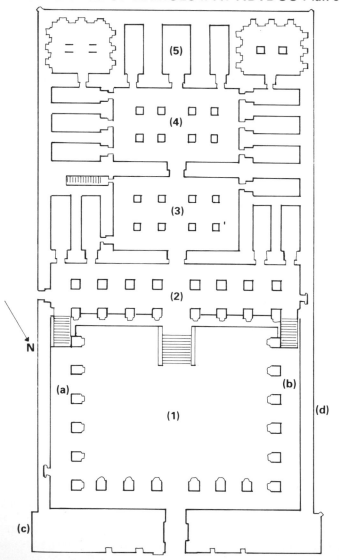

sill of red granite. The two sculptured panels represent Ramses embracing Osiris.

As with all Egyptian temples, the temple of Ramses II was completely decorated, both inside and out. The walls on the inside were covered with religious subject matter: scenes of priests bearing flowers and sacrificial animals towards the temple; and processions of people singing, clapping hands, blowing trumpets and carrying banners. On the outside walls there were scenes of official journeys, wars and activities abroad.

A typical religious scene may be found in the **Second Court** (1) on the right-hand wall (a), where a procession of servants bear dishes of food on their heads; it is preceded by a priest burning incense in front of a statuette of the king that is borne on the shoulders of the leading priest. The scribe of the temple records the offerings received by another priest. On the left-hand wall (b) are butchers, slaughtering and cutting up sacrificial bulls. Servants run forward with the joints of meat. Each piece is purified by a priest who carries a vase of libation water.

The surviving battle scenes on the *outside* of the temple can be found on the eastern face of the northern tower (c) and the western wall (d). These are not in good condition, and will be but briefly described.

The scene at (c), from left to right, shows the text of the battle (1) that differs from that at Abu Simbel by a special decree that Ramses' two chariot horses should be commended for their bravery by henceforth receiving food in his presence for ever. Ramses II is depicted in his chariot (2) with Egyptian soldiers beneath him (3).

Ramses II at Abydos; outer wall of temple (c)

He watches scribes who count and record the hands of the slain enemy (4) and prisoners of war (5). The Hittite army and camp are depicted (6), with Ramses surrounded by the enemy (7). The great battle scene is to the right (8) showing Hittite chariots, the Hittites rescuing their friends from the river Orontes into which they were driven, and the king of Aleppo being held upside down to disgorge water.

The scene on the western wall (d) shows (from left to right) hand-to-hand combat between Hittites, Egyptian and Sherdan soldiers; Ramses' camp protected by infantry carrying shields; Ramses' chariot, with sunshade and with groom holding the reigns; and the Egyptian infantry and chariots.

All representations of Ramses II, unlike those of his father Seti I, are proud, arrogant, and confident. His head is always held high and his shoulders are squared.

A CONCEPT OF THE AFTERLIFE

According to some of the mortuary texts, the afterlife lay beyond a gap in the mountains to the west of Abydos. It was depicted as a long mountainous valley with a river running through it; the banks were lined with wheat fields, fruit orchards and gardens of flowers. Here the deceased would enjoy hunting and fishing forever and ever.

Osiris as Lord of the Underworld (see page 88)

Temple of Ramses II at Abydos: Sherdan soldiers

34

MAP OF ASWAN AND ENVIRONS Plan 6

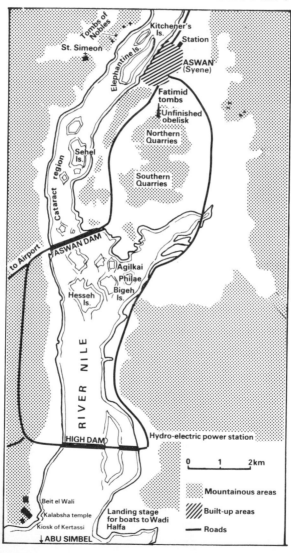

Tombs of Nobles

Kitchener's Is.

Station

St. Simeon

ASWAN (Syene)

Elephantine Is.

Fatimid tombs

Unfinished obelisk

Northern Quarries

Sehel Is.

Cataract region

Southern Quarries

to Airport

ASWAN DAM

Agilkai

Philae

Bigeh Is.

Hesseh Is.

RIVER NILE

HIGH DAM

Hydro-electric power station

0 1 2km

Beit el Wali

Kalabsha temple

Kiosk of Kertassi

↓ABU SIMBEL

Landing stage for boats to Wadi Halfa

▓ Mountainous areas

▨ Built-up areas

— Roads

CHAPTER 2 ASWAN (SYENE)

BACKGROUND

The Greek word *Syene* (from which the Coptic *Suan* is derived) stems from the ancient Egyptian *Swenet*, meaning 'making business' or trade. And herein lies the character of Aswan. It has been a flourishing borderline market for thousands of years; the link between two cultures: Egyptian and Nubian.

The surrounding land was rich in building materials: the Aswan quarries were the source of fine and coarse quality granite from whence builders and sculptors throughout ancient Egyptian history drew their supplies. Quartz, which was used for polishing stone, was mined from the so-called alabaster quarry north of Aswan and also from the western desert. In the eastern desert there were iron mines where red ochre was extracted for paint. And the largest sandstone quarry in Egypt was situated at Silsilla, further northwards.

Feluccas on the Nile near the Old Cataract Hotel

In antiquity the island of Elephantine was known as *Abu* or Elephant Land. It commanded the Nile cataracts that formed a natural boundary to the south. These great granite-toothed boulders had been tugged and torn from the mother rock by countless floods and lay like huge obstacles on the river-bed. At low Nile a sluggish river would wind a sinuous six-kilometre descent from the island of Hesseh to Aswan. When the water began to swell with the annual flood, however, the river's mood would become restless. Confined by mountain ranges on each side of the valley, the river would dance or whip around the granite obstructions. Fed by the monsoons on the Ethiopian tableland, the Nile would continue to rise until, reeling and rushing, churning and roaring in agony to find an outlet, it would hurl into the channels of Aswan. Classical writers described the sound as so great as to cause deafness.

Granite boulders of the cataract region

The Gods of the Inundation
To the ancient Egyptians a tradition survived from their remote past, that the cataract region was the edge of the world. It was said that here the life-giving waters (the annual inundation) rose from the primaeval ocean Nun to render the land fertile. Welcoming the chocolate-brown flood was Hapi the Nile-god. He was believed to

live in a grotto at Bigeh Island, and his role was a dual one: receiving the waters with oustretched arms and directing its flow into the eternal ocean (the Mediterranean) in the north. Hapi was depicted as a simple fisherman or oarsman with a narrow belt and the bulbous breasts of plenty. On his head were aquatic plants: the papyrus symbolised his role as giver of water to Lower Egypt and the lotus to Upper Egypt. Hapi came to represent the provinces of Egypt in temple reliefs, offering the fruits of the land to the great god to whom a temple was dedicated.

Having received the 'first water', Hapi left it to two guardian goddesses of the cataracts to control and direct the flood. Anukis, on the island of Sehel and portrayed with a lofty head-dress of feathers, clasped the river banks and compressed the swirling waters, directing it towards Aswan. Satis, on the island of Elephantine, let fly the current with the force of an arrow; she is usually depicted carrying a bow and arrows. Khnum, the ram-headed god, was the great god of the whole of the cataract region, and hence of the inundation. In the company of his wife Satis and daughter Anukis, Khnum received manifold offerings at his sanctuary on Elephantine. Famines due to low flood were attributed to his anger at insufficient offerings. In fact, Khnum later became the focus of an elaborate tradition in which he was not only a god of the inundation but also a god of creation, having fashioned man on a potter's wheel from the clay of the river.

Elephantine was inhabited from very early times. A tribe bearing an elephant emblem settled there in pre-history and erected the first shrine to Khnum. On their heavily fortified island home, where they commanded a good view of the surrounding landscape, they were safe from surprise raids. Opposite the northern end of the island lay Aswan, the trading centre on the mainland. Thus, while peace had not yet been made with the Nubian tribes on the border and a state of uncertainty prevailed, products were exchanged.

'Keepers of the Southern Gate'

Though Aswan was situated at the farthest limit of Egypt, it was spiritually closer to the capital of Memphis than any other city. This was because, during the Old Kingdom, the noblemen of Elephantine were the 'Keepers of the Southern Gate'; Aswan was the starting point for the caravan routes along which the earliest commercial and later military expeditions were carried out. The noblemen held extremely responsible positions. They were entrusted with supervising the quarrying of granite for the great monuments of the Giza plateau. They watched over the exchange of Egyptian grain and oil for minerals, ebony, gum, stone beads, incense, and animal skins from the south. They supervised the shipments to the royal capital.

The noblemen of Elephantine were a proud and independent breed who lived at a time when the pharaoh encouraged initiative and responsible action; a time when many Lower Egyptians travelled to Upper Egypt to find work, just as, today, Upper Egyptians travel to the Delta.

Aswan attained its greatest political prestige in the 6th Dynasty (2345–2181 BC). The tombs of the noblemen at Kubbet el Hawa (page 41) have autobiographical texts that show them to have been administrators, warriors and explorers as well as politicians.

One nobleman called Hekaib ('Brave of Heart') appears to have had all these qualities and more. In fact, he was so widely respected that, after his death, he was revered by noblemen and high priests for no less than eight generations. Over two centuries after his death, a prince of Elephantine in the reign of the pharaoh Senusert I, finally constructed a sanctuary in Hekaib's name on Elephantine. This sanctuary was discovered in 1946 by Labib Habachi, who noted that never before had such honour been paid to an ordinary man. Habachi was able to identify the deified Hekaib with Pepi-Nakht, from whose tomb (page 43) we learn that he was respected for a distinguished career and an aggressive spirit as well as for bravery. For example, at that time ships were built on the eastern end of the caravan route from Coptos, and a naval officer on duty there was slaughtered by nomads. The pharaoh chose one of his most competent officials to rescue the body and punish the offenders. It was Hekaib, and he so fearlessly chastised the troublemakers that he was later described as 'one who controlled his heart when others stayed at home'.

It is not surprising that the noblemen of Elephantine were among the first to try and shake off the restraint of the central government and establish independence towards the end of the Old Kingdom. Unfortunately, it was a short-lived achievement, soon to be followed by chaos and civil war.

Aswan's time of glory was over. It was never again to have such prestige. An effort was made in the Middle Kingdom to resuscitate the spirit by reviving Old Kingdom titles such as 'Governor of the South'. But, in fact, Aswan had lost its role as Gateway to the South when Egyptian influence spread into Nubia (2133 BC). The high priests of Elephantine watched over the Temple of Khnum and continued to promote the cult of Hekaib, but Aswan was, in fact, no more than a military base and an emporium for Nubian and African exotica.

Some pharaohs of later periods constructed temples on Elephantine, as can be seen from numerous reused blocks, but it was not until the Graeco-Roman period that Aswan regained its importance, and then for very different reasons.

During the reign of Ptolemy II (285–246 BC) the popular cults of Osiris, Isis and Horus were transferred from Abydos to the area around Aswan, and particularly the cataract region immediately to the south of Elephantine. The regional gods of the cataracts, Khnum the ram-headed god with his wife Satis and daughter Anukis, were supplanted by the triad from Abydos. The chief centre for the worship of Isis became the Island of Philae which gained a mystical aura. The temple of Isis soon came to be regarded as the holiest in the land, especially famed for the mysterious healing properties of the goddess.

Early sightseers
Greeks, Macedonians, Carians, Romans, and Egyptians travelled to Aswan. All fell under the spell of its beauty. Strabo the Roman geographer, Ibn Khaldun the historian-diplomat of mediaeval times, Shelley and Keates the nineteenth-century romantics and countless others succumbed to the legendary river, its fabled ruins, and the healthy climate and breathtaking sunsets of Aswan.

Among the people who left their mark at Aswan were Sir F. Grenfell who, before starting his campaign in the Sudan, took time to clear many of the rock tombs at Kubbet el Hawa (1885–86), Lady Cecil, the wife of a diplomat, who also cleared a tomb, and Lord Kitchener, who imported and planted a large variety of African and Indian plants on one of the islands.

Lady Duff Gordon set a fashion when she travelled to Upper Egypt to seek a cure for tuberculosis. After her, came many of Europe's notables who sought a retreat from Europe's cruel winter. They journeyed slowly up the Nile in plush-fitted river vessels that were not much different from those used by the ancient pharaohs and successive Roman, Arab and Ottoman visitors before them. The pink and purple hills in the distance, pierced by a honeycomb of tombs, were yet unexplored. The temples of the pharaohs, their colonnades lying broken or askew, where half-buried in the sand. Luxor had yielded but a small part of its great treasure. Aswan languished in its depôt-like tradition. The island of Philae had not yet been engulfed by the waters behind the Aswan Dam. Elephantine and 'Kitchener Island' were so fertile that, according to tradition, grapes grew on them all the year round.

DESCRIPTION

Elephantine Island

This island, which was once of such strategic importance and great renown, is of little touristic interest. The ruins near the quay are all that remain of two New Kingdom Temples that were destroyed by a ruler in 1821 who disliked tourists coming to see them!

The **Museum**, which contains antiquities excavated from Aswan and its environs and from Nubia, was first built as a resting place for those engaged on building the original Aswan Dam. The exhibits include miscellaneous pre-dynastic objects recovered from Nubia before it was inundated, some Old and Middle Kingdom objects, especially from the Hekaib Sanctuary, various objects of the New Kingdom, and discoveries of the Graeco-Roman period; the latter include mummies of a priest and priestess of Philae found on the Island of Hesseh, and a mummy of the sacred ram.

Plans are under way to build a new museum at Aswan to house these and other selected pieces from Nubia that are now in Cairo Museum. Meanwhile, many of the most important pieces are stored.

Nilometer at Elephantine

An ancient **Nilometer** faces Aswan. It consists of a stairway on the river's bank constructed of regular-shaped stones; it was so designed that the water, rising and falling with the ebb and flow of the flood, could register maximum, minimum and average water levels. A text inscribed on a wall of the Temple of Edfu tells us that when the river rose to 24 cubits and $3\frac{1}{2}$ hands at Elephantine, there was sufficient water to supply the needs of the whole country. Plutarch, the Greek writer, recorded that the Nile once rose at Elephantine to a height of 28 cubits (14.70 metres).

The Nilometer was repaired by the Khedive Ismail in 1870. He recorded his work in both French and Arabic. A new scale was established and the ancient construction, unused for centuries, came into use once more. On the walls of the staircase are records in Demotic (fluid hieroglyphic hand) and Greek, showing different water levels.

A second Nilometer, dating to the 26th Dynasty, was recently found by the German-Swiss Institutes of Archaeology, who have been excavating and reconstructing the ruins of the **Old Town**, at the southern tip of the island, for the last twelve years. Among the monuments there are a granite portal, which once formed the entrance to a large temple, and which is one of few structures in the Nile valley with reliefs of Alexander IV, the son of Alexander the Macedonian conqueror, by Roxane; and the foundations of a small temple built by Nektanebos II, the last native pharaoh, Julius Caesar and Trajan (98–117 AD), whose inscription survives on the single remaining stump of column. Blocks from the edifices of earlier temples with inscriptions of Thutmose III, Ramses III and other New Kingdom pharaohs, had been reused in this temple, and also in another temple of Satis.

ROCK TOMBS OF KUBBET EL HAWA
(WESTERN BANK)

All were broken into at an early date and are not easy of access to the average tourist.

The Kubbet el Hawa, or Dome of the Wind, takes its name from the tiny tomb of a sheikh that rises in lonely silhouette on the summit of the hill almost opposite the northern end of Elephantine. Beneath it, cut into the rock face of the cliff, are the tombs of the noblemen of Elephantine.

6TH DYNASTY TOMBS (2345–2181 BC)

The autobiographical texts inscribed on these tombs relate to administrative abilities and show a pioneering spirit; expeditions were made into the then unknown upper-cataract region. The noblemen declare themselves to be men of high moral character, and recorded how they fed the hungry, clothed the needy, and spoke 'only that which was good'. The texts also reveal filial devotion:

Mekhu was a nobleman of Elephantine in the reign of Pepi II. He held the title Governor of the South. While on an expedition in Wawat (Lower Nubia) his convoy was attacked by desert tribes, and he was killed. When his son Sabni received the news of his father's death, he quickly mustered a convoy of troops and pack-donkeys to march southwards and recover the body. He informed the pharaoh of his intention and recorded his experience in his tomb, which adjoins the one he built for his father.

Tomb of Sabni (No. 26)
Sabni's text relates how he travelled to Wawat and duly punished the tribe responsible for his father's death. Then he recovered the body and started his journey home. Meanwhile, his sovereign, Pepi II, had despatched a whole convoy of royal embalmers and mortuary priests along with the necessary oils and linens for mummification and internment. Such honour paid to a nobleman of Elephantine confirms the close ties between Memphis, the capital, and Aswan, the Southern Gate. In an expression of gratitude Sabni later set out for Memphis to hand over to Pepi Mekhu's rich cargo.

The entrance to Sabni's tomb is unusually divided by a cross beam. The lower section forms the actual doorway and the upper section a window. The tomb chamber, which has fourteen square pillars, is of no special interest, apart from a relief on the rear wall that shows the deceased hunting from a boat in the company of his daughters. This is an appealing representation combining action and sensitivity. Sabni holds the javelin in his right hand and the slain birds in his left. To the right, he harpoons two fish at a single strike. At the centre, birds take to the air above a papyrus thicket.

The Tomb of Mekhu (No. 25)
This tomb, built by Sabni for his father, comprises a single chamber, crude in both construction and decoration. There are eighteen roughly hewn columns, in three rows. A stone table or

shrine with three legs is situated between the two columns facing the entrance. Representations on the walls and columns are poor. They show the deceased receiving various offerings. To the left of the entrance is a rural scene of ploughing and tilling of the land and donkeys laden with the harvest. The stele on the rear wall, opposite the entrance, is in a recess approached by steps.

Tomb of Harkhuf (No. 34)

Harkhuf was an explorer, and his tomb contains lengthy descriptions of his pioneering expeditions; three were made in the reign of Merenre, and one in the reign of his successor, Pepi II.

Harkhuf called himself 'caravan-leader' and journeyed with pack-donkeys beyond the Second Cataract. His first journey took seven months. His second appears to have been even more adventurous and he was proud to record that 'never had any companion or caravan-leader . . . done it before'. Each time he brought back precious products. Harkhuf had trouble on his third expedition. Some desert tribes were warring with one another, and Harkhuf became involved. He reduced the *Temehu* (a tribe related to the Libyans) to subjection and so impressed the Nubian chiefs that they offered him guides and cattle for his return journey.

On his fourth expedition Harkhuf brought back gold, ostrich feathers, animal skins, ivory, ebony, incense and gum. He also brought a 'dancing pygmy' for his pharaoh, the young Pepi II, who came to the throne at the age of six. In his record, Harkhuf states that he sent his messengers ahead of his convoy to inform His Majesty of his gift, to which Pepi wrote back in his great enthusiasm that the pygmy should be guarded night and day so as not to fall overboard. Harkhuf was so proud of the letter that he had it engraved on the façade of his tomb.

Tomb of Pepi-Nakht, called Hekaib (No. 35)

This is the tomb of the deified Elephantine nobleman, whose sanctuary was built on Elephantine, and who was honoured by no less than eight generations. His tomb is in poor condition, but his autobiographical text, recorded on each side of the entrance doorway, enables us to trace his activities.

Pepi-Nakht conducted several campaigns into Lower Nubia. On one occasion, he suppressed a rebellion and returned with captives, including the children of the chiefs as hostages. On another occasion, he brought back two Nubian chiefs themselves in order to talk matters over with the Egyptians and come to an amicable settlement. Pepi-Nakht also had a confrontation on the Red Sea coast when he and his troop force slew large numbers of 'sand-dwellers'; this was in retaliation against the bedouin tribes that had killed a certain Enenkhet and his men, who were building a ship on the Red Sea coast with which to sail to Punt. Pepi-Nakht returned to the Nile valley with the body of the deceased nobleman.

TOMBS OF THE MIDDLE KINGDOM (*c.* 1980–1920 BC)

Tomb of Sirenput I (No. 36)
Sirenput was a prince of Elephantine in the reign of Senusert I, at the beginning of the Middle Kingdom. It was he who was encouraged by his sovereign to erect the sanctuary of Hekaib, and the royal artists he entrusted with the work on the sanctuary also decorated his own tomb.

The façade is carefully and finely sculpted. Sirenput is shown in seated position at the top of the staircase. Behind is a court with six pillars, all bearing representations of him. On the rear wall (left) is a large relief showing him followed by his sandal-bearer and two dogs, and hunting in the marsh (above). Cattle, including some angry bulls, are brought to him. To the right, he is seated in a colonnade with four women: his wife, mother and two daughters who bear him flowers.

Tomb of Sirenput II (No. 31)
This tomb, belonging to the grandson of Sirenput I, who was a prince in the reigns of Amenemhet II and Senusert II, is one of the most well-preserved of the Middle Kingdom. It is entered through a courtyard leading to a narrow passage, an excavated hall with six elegant square undecorated columns, and a corridor with three recesses on each side, each containing a statue of the deceased sculpted from the living rock.

The small hall at the end of the corridor has four pillars and a recess at the rear. The condition of the reliefs in the recess is excellent, both the delicately worked hieroglyphics and the delightful family scenes. To the rear, the deceased is seated at a table. His son stands before him bearing flowers. On the right-hand wall is a representation of his mother seated at a table with the deceased to her right. On the left-hand wall is a similar scene with his wife and son.

Granite Quarries (Eastern Bank)

Situated in the eastern desert, directly to the south of Aswan, are the ancient quarries of granite in hues of red, yellow, brown and dark grey. Sculptors and builders for thousands of years drew their supplies from here.

The earliest pharaoh to exploit the quarry was Den of the 1st Dynasty, who used blocks for the floor of his cenotaph at Abydos. The 2nd Dynasty pharaoh Khasekhemui used it for his fine temple at Nekhen (Hierakonopolis). Then, in the Old Kingdom the quarry was fully exploited, especially by the 4th Dynasty pharaohs who raised their monuments at Giza: nine great slabs of fifty-four tons each were extracted from the quarries for the ceiling of the so-called King's Chamber of the Pyramid of Khufu (Cheops). Red granite was chosen for the Valley, or Granite, Temple of Khafre (Chephren). Black granite was quarried and despatched for the lower reaches of the outer casing of the Pyramid of Menkaure (Mycerinus). Thenceforth, right through to Graeco-Roman times, the quarry was in use.

Many blocks were abandoned in various stages of completion, which enables us to see the process by which the stone was extracted. Holes were bored along a prescribed straight line. It was once thought that wooden wedges were driven into these, watered and left to expand until it split the stone. Recent excavations, however, have changed our understanding of the quarrying industry. Balls of dolerite, the hardest of stone, weighing up to five-and-a-half kilogrammes, have been found in their hundreds in the area of the quarry, and it is now believed that these were attached to rammers and simultaneously struck with great force by the quarry workers. They were also used to pound and dress the surface of the stone.

The system must have been reasonably sure because blocks were very often decorated on three sides before being detached from the natural rock.

The huge **Unfinished Obelisk**, lying in the northern quarry, is still attached to the bedrock. The reason for its abandonment is that flaws were found in the stone. An attempt was then made to extract smaller obelisks from it, but these projects, too, were abandoned. There is no indication for whom it was intended. The only marks on the surface are those of the workmen. Had it ever been completed, it would have weighed some 1,162 tons and have soared to a height of forty-two metres.

In the southern quarry, rough-hewn blocks show that statues and

46

sarcophagi were roughly shaped before transportation in order to cut down the weight. In the case of the former, the sculptor would begin to hew out the feet at a point several inches above the base of the rock, leaving the lower segment as firm support for the figure. In this quarry there are two rough-shaped sarcophagi that date to the Graeco-Roman period, a rock bearing an inscription of Amenhotep III, and an unfinished colossus of a king (or Osiris) grasping a crook and flail.

OTHER SITES AT ASWAN

Mausoleum of the Aga Khan
The late Aga Khan III, leader of the Ismaili community, a sect of Islam, found such peace and beauty in Aswan that before he died in 1957 he chose a site on the western bank of the Nile, on a peak overlooking his favourite part of the river, for his tomb. His Mausoleum, built in the Fatimid style with a single dome, is a landmark of Aswan today. It stands cool and isolated on an area of 450 square metres. It is constructed of rose granite, and the inner walls are of marble embellished with verses from the Koran. The Aga Khan claimed direct descent from Fatimah, the daughter of the prophet Mohammad. The tombs of the Fatimids are on the eastern bank of the Nile (see Map No. 6)

Tomb of the Aga Khan

The Aswan Dam

For thousands of years, leadership in Egypt has been associated with that great source of life – the Nile. From the first pharaoh, Narmer (3100 BC), who traditionally diverted the river at Memphis, to Nektanebos (360 BC), the last Egyptian pharaoh, canals were cleared and irrigation projects were carried out. When the Persians conquered Egypt they repaired waterways. The Greeks reclaimed land. The Romans built aqueducts. The Mamluks constructed aqueducts and storage systems.

In 1842 the Mohamed Aly Barrage was built at the apex of the Delta north of Cairo. This first barrage was followed by others: at Aswan, Esna, and Assiut. The first Aswan Dam was constructed between 1899–1902. It was raised in 1907–1912, and again in 1929–1934, at which time 5,000 million cubic metres of water was stored in a reservoir that backed upstream to Wadi Halfa.

The High Dam (Saad el Aali)

The High Dam, situated six-and-a-half kilometres south of the Aswan Dam, was the cornerstone of the country's economic development envisioned by Gamal Abdel Nasser. It was built during the years 1960–71 and was largely financed and supervised by the Soviet Union after the withdrawal of US and British financial aid for the project. Thirty thousand Egyptians worked on shifts day and night for ten years, under the supervision of two thousand technicians. A total of 17,000,000 cubic metres of rock was excavated, and 42,700,000 cubic metres of construction material was used.

The High Dam is a rock-filled dam – an artificial mountain of earth and rock over a cement and clay core. It is 3,600 metres long, 114 metres high, and the width at the base is 980 metres. The diversion tunnels on the western bank of the river (each with a diameter of sixteen-and-a-half metres), were hewn out of granite to a length of 1,950 metres. On the eastern bank are the High Dam's twelve turbines, each with 120,000 HP. The annual hydro-electric capacity is ten billion KW hours.

High Dam lake was formed when the thwarted Nile swelled back upon itself for hundreds of kilometres where Nubia once stood. It is the world's largest artificial lake. It extends for over 500 kilometres, 150 of which are in Sudanese territory. The average width is ten kilometres, and there are areas where it spreads across thirty kilometres. The storage capacity is 157 billion cubic metres.

Advantages The primary purpose of the High Dam is to expand Egypt's arable land, provide hydro-electric power for the benefit of industrial development, and ensure a substantial rise in the standard of living. Due to this long-term storage of water, regular irrigation is possible, and Egypt's productivity has been increased by over twenty per cent: from 800,000 hectares of reclaimed desert land, and from the increased yield resulting from the change-over from a one-crop to a three-crop cycle. The latter was made possible by the stabilisation of the river, which overcomes the danger of high and low floods and also enables permanent navigability.

The loss of silt has been compensated for by fertilizer, one of the many industries provided with hydro-electric power from the dam. Another industry is a shale brick factory that will replace the age-old brick made of Nile silt.

Disadvantages An increase in the arable land has led to a corresponding increase in the incidence of bilharzia which can now, fortunately, be controlled. Predatory fish from the Red Sea, no longer hindered by the fresh water flow that acted as a barrier, have been seen in the Mediterranean for the first time; the resulting loss to fisheries is partly compensated by a large fishing industry on the Lake. The loss of the annual flood, and the constant higher average water level, has resulted in increased salinity of the soil. This has affected crops and ancient monuments; the agricultural land, especially in the Delta, now requires constant irrigation and drainage; and the ancient monuments of Upper Egypt are suffering some damage from seepage and salt erosion.

The most tragic loss has, of course, been Nubia. No less than 100,000 persons had to be uprooted and relocated in Upper Egypt and the Sudan when plans for the High Dam went ahead and it was clear that their homes were destined to disappear forever. Ironically, it is due to the disappearance of Nubia that we know more about its history than we do of many sites in Egypt, including Luxor! For, during the years 1960–69, the doomed land was subject to the most concentrated archaeological operations ever mounted. Scholars, engineers, architects, and photographers from over thirty countries fought against time, and some great monuments were saved (page 146) or documented for future study. Countless objects were excavated and removed to safety. However, much of Nubia's heritage in the form of towns, tombs, temples, churches, graffiti and inscriptions, has been engulfed by the waters.

Outdated traditions and rural continuum

The age-old tradition of prosperity or adversity being dependent on
the Nile flood and the fervour with which the Nile festivals were
celebrated, has finally run its course. It was started thousands of
years ago by the earliest settlers of the Nile valley who thought that
rites, spells, and offerings of thanks would control, appease, or
please the power behind natural phenomena. In earliest times a bull
or goose, and later a roll of papyrus, written with sacred words,
would be cast on the waters.

The eruption of the river and the subsequent blossoming of the
land was regarded as the result of a marriage. Even after the Arab
conquest, public criers walking the streets announced the progress
of the flood, so that the *qadi* could prepare a 'contract of marriage'.
The Bride of the Nile Ceremony took place, during which a
symbolic maiden would be given to the river. Witnesses confirmed
the 'consummation' and, with elaborate oriental ceremonial, the
dykes were broken. Until the 1970s, the arrival of the flood was the
occasion for a public holiday, and a procession of garlanded boats
filled with rejoicing people cast flowers upon the waters.

Today it is no longer necessary to please Hapi, the Nile-god. The
water is released by sluices operated at man's will, and the thirsty
land quenches itself to man's timetable. The Nile no longer
revitalises the soil with its rich alluvium. The Black Land, *Kmt*,
which was the name for Egypt, is deprived of its natural source of
fertility.

But continuity survives change, and in Upper Egypt one can best
see the apparent paradox of Egypt undergoing repeated change, yet
remaining changeless. Though new hotels, factories, and highways
reflect the modern era, we can still see the simple village with dust
roads and rectangular mud-brick houses. There are transport
vehicles on the one hand, and the faithful donkeys as the beast of
burden, on the other. Tractors and modern equipment are used
alongside the time-honoured plough and the *shaduf*, the most ancient
of pumping devices for lifting water from the river to the canals.

Monuments of Nubia reconstructed near the High Dam:
Temple of Kalabsha and rock inscriptions (page 141)
Temple of Beit el Wali (page 145)
Kiosk of Kertassi (page 146)
Graeco-Roman Monuments:
The Island of Philae (page 183)
Monastery of St Simeon (page 211)

50

LUXOR Plan 7

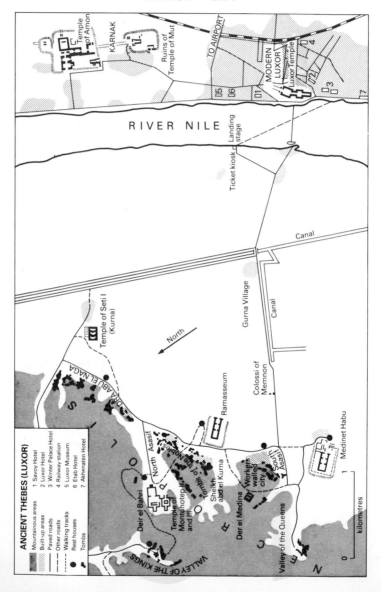

RIVER NILE

Temple of Amon

KARNAK

Ruins of Temple of Mut

TO AIRPORT

MODERN LUXOR

Luxor Temple

4

2

3

7

15

16

01

Landing stage

Ticket kiosk

Canal

Canal

Gurna Village

Temple of Seti I (Kurna)

North

DRA ABU EL NAGA

S

North Asasif

Temple of the Nobles

Ramasseum

Colossi of Memnon

Medinet Habu

Deir el Bahri

Temple of Montuhotep II and III

Tombs of the Nobles

Sheikh abd el Kurna

South Asasif

Workers walled city

Deir el Medina

Valley of the Queens

VALLEY OF THE KINGS

N

ANCIENT THEBES (LUXOR)
1 Savoy Hotel
2 Luxor Hotel
3 Winter Palace Hotel
4 Railway station
5 Luxor Museum
6 Etab Hotel
7 Akhenaten Hotel

Mountainous areas
Built-up areas
Paved roads
Other roads
Walking tracks
Rest houses
Tombs

kilometres

1

0

CHAPTER 3   LUXOR (THEBES)

BACKGROUND

Perhaps no city in the world has bequeathed to us more numerous nor mightier monuments than Thebes. The ancient city stood on both sides of the Nile, and few spots in Egypt are so ideally suited to such a purpose. The range of hills to the east and west curve away from the river's bank leaving broad plains on either side. Here marvellous monuments were raised in honour of Amon-Ra.

Potter's shop in the village of Luxor

Luxor, which developed into the great capital of the Egyptian empire, had no particular importance during the first thousand years of Egypt's ancient history. When Narmer moved northwards to unite the Two Lands and establish Memphis as capital; in the Early Dynastic Period when the kings constructed their cenotaphs at Abydos; during the Great Pyramid Age when granite was quarried from Aswan in the south and transported to the necropolis of Giza to the north — throughout all these long centuries Luxor was no different from the chief cities of other provinces.

It was only after the collapse of the Old Kingdom, when the country had passed through the period of disorder known as the First Intermediate Period, that a noble family from Armant, a village south of Luxor, began to assert themselves. They had already shown their powers of leadership by distributing grain between various provinces in times of low flood, and towards the end of the 10th Dynasty (2133 BC), they annexed Luxor and moved north-wards. Their aim was to reunite the Two Lands and take over leadership.

At this time another powerful family from the Fayoum area ruled from Memphis to Assiut, and aware of the aspirations of the Theban family, they moved their forces to meet them. The result was a long and bitter struggle. However, the Thebans emerged victorious, reunited the Two Lands, and launched Egypt on its second great period: the Middle Kingdom.

For some two centuries (1991–1786 BC) Egypt enjoyed a period of peace and prosperity. Luxor, however, was capital for only a short time before the pharaohs chose a site more suitable for a central government: El Lisht, some thirty kilometres south of Memphis. Political stability led to an art and architectural revival, important irrigation projects, and extensive commerce with neighbouring lands. Egyptian influence spread to Libya, Crete, Palestine, Syria, and southwards to Nubia where great fortresses were built (page 127). The most significant event in Luxor, however, was the introduction of the god Amon-Ra and the building of modest shrines in his honour.

It was only after the Hyksos occupation and expulsion that Luxor and its local god achieved prestige, and then on a scale never imagined. For, after the Thebans (Kamose followed by his brother Ahmose, father of the New Kingdom) won the war of liberation, they not only drove the hated occupiers out of Egypt but swore to avenge their country for its suffering. They followed the enemy into Asia, and the age of conquest began.

The New Kingdom (1567–1080 BC) was the empire period. Thutmose I extended Egypt's southern border towards Kush (page 128), and Thutmose III established Egyptian supremacy in Asia Minor and all the neighbouring countries. As trade flourished, Luxor became paramount among the cities of Egypt. Caravans from the conquered territories, laden with gold and silver, precious metals, ivory, timber, spices, rare flora and fauna, made their way to Upper Egypt.

The priests of Amon-Ra, into whose hands a vast portion of the wealth was pouring acquired increasing influence, and the pharaohs ordered the construction of marvellous monuments in honour of their god. They declared that Amon-Ra was not only 'God of Karnak' and 'God of Thebes', but was, in fact, the 'King of Gods', and that their priesthood was second to none.

Age of Glory and Discontent

Though the 18th Dynasty was an age of unparalleled grandeur, it was also a period of transition. Old values were passing and new ones were emerging. The spirit of the age of glory, wealth and power. But, there was grave discontent among the upper classes. Though temples were built in honour of Amon-Ra by Hatshepsut, Thutmose III and Amenhotep III, there was criticism of the national god and the materialism of the priests who promoted his cult. Egypt's tradition-bound intellectuals watched with apprehension the growing power of the priesthood that had elevated a once obscure deity to the rank of national god.

It was in this atmosphere that Amenhotep IV (Akhenaten) grew up. His worship of a single god, the sun's disc, the Aten, was both a revolution and an attempt to bring back a more purified form of sun worship (Chapter 4). The movement affected a small minority. The ideal of a religious community isolated at Tel el Amarna, and the practical requirements of governing an empire were not compatible. After the deaths of Akhenaten and his half-brother Smenkare, Tutankhaten came to the throne and the priests of Amon made a great spectacle of their return to power.

Tutankhaten's name was changed to Tutankhamon, and in an elaborate ceremony the young king appeared before the rejoicing public. Thebes had not known such pageantry for many years, and it was clear that the priests could hardly contain their pleasure. The city was bedecked with ribbons and flags. Standard-bearers marched in the streets. Dancers, singers, drummers and acrobats lined the banks of the river. The population came from miles around to hear that 'Amon loved better than his son . . . Tutankhamon, he who satisfies all the gods'.

The great and prosperous 18th Dynasty, which had started with such high hope under such pharaohs as Ahmose (who rid the country of the Hyksos), Thutmose III (who established an Egyptian empire) and Amenhotep III (who ruled the state at the peak of its glory), had ended in halting recovery from the religious movement of Akhenaten. Haremhab, the general who seized the throne at the end of the 18th Dynasty, was an excellent administrator who re-established a strong government and started a programme of restoration. This was continued in the 19th Dynasty when the pharaohs channelled their boundless energies into reorganising the army after its disastrous setbacks during Akhenaten's rule. Seti I fought battles against the Libyans, Syrians and Hittites, and he raised large temples at Karnak, Kurna (on the necropolis of Thebes) and Abydos. Ramses II waged wars against the Hittites, culmina-ting in his well documented Battle of Kadesh. And Ramses III successfully protected his country from the 'People of the Sea' who were most probably Sardinians.

Though turning their attention to salvaging the empire, the pharaohs did not neglect national affairs. With wealth pouring into the state capital, they all tried to outdo one another in the magnificence of their monuments.

Theban Decline
During the reigns of Ramses IV–XI, the country fell more and more under the control of the priests of Amon-Ra. As their power grew, they demanded blind conformity to a system that gave them control and their temples wealth. The demand for gold and workers to mine it, the need for troops for the almost continuous war in Asia, and the independence of the powerful leaders in Nubia and Kush weighed heavily on the state. A power struggle was inevitable.

By the reign of Ramses IX there was such disorder that Hrihor, High Priest of Amon, was able to declare himself to be Viceroy of Kush. This combination of religious and secular power enabled him (1085 BC) to usurp the throne of the pharaohs. Egypt became a land divided. Lower Egypt was ruled by a Dynasty in Tanis in the Delta. Upper Egypt was ruled by Hrihor. Both kingdoms were so weakened that a powerful Dynasty of Libyan descent was able to take over control of the country. Palestine and Syria were lost. Nubia, where many Upper Egyptians had taken refuge, gained independence.

While Egypt was sinking into mediocrity, deep in the heart of Kush a pharaonic style court continued. Though African in origin, it was Egyptian in tradition and belief. The king bore pharaonic titles, and the cult of Amon-Ra had long been established there. Aware that Egypt was torn by dissention, these proud and vigorous

Kushite rulers marched northwards to put an end to the prevailing corruption and re-establish order.

Under the Kushite leaders, Egypt enjoyed a period of internal stability. Temples were restored and age-old texts were reinscribed. However, their role in Egypt came to an end with the Assyrian conquest, when all Egypt's great cities, especially Thebes, were mercilessly sacked. After the Assyrians came a short-lived revival, known as the Saite period, followed by the Persian invasions and then the Greek and Roman occupations, when the wonders of 'Hundred-gated Thebes' spread throughout the Graeco-Roman world

It is perhaps a measure of the greatness of Thebes that Libyans, Kushites, Greeks and Romans honoured, embellished and adorned the ancient city.

DESCRIPTION

Temple of Luxor

This beautiful temple was built on the east bank of the Nile by Amenhotep III, 'The Magnificent'. With his wife Queen Tiy, whom he dearly loved, he ruled Egypt during the peaceful and stable 18th Dynasty. The temple was dedicated to the Theban triad: the great god Amon-Ra, his wife Mut, and their son Khonsu.

Statue of Ramses II in the Great Court (A) of Luxor Temple

56

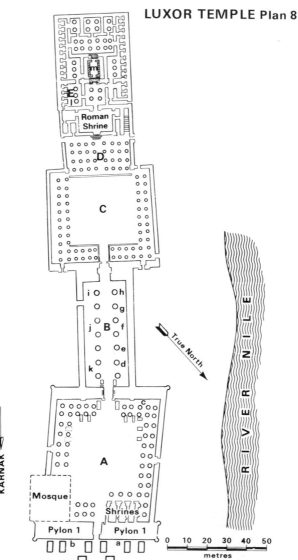

LUXOR TEMPLE Plan 8

m

E

Roman
Shrine

D

C

i O   O h

O O g

j O B O f

O   O e

k O O d

O   O c

KARNAK

Mosque

Shrines

Pylon 1   Pylon 1

b   a

True North

R I V E R   N I L E

0   10   20   30   40   50

metres

57

Luxor temple suffered some damage in the reign of Amenhotep's son Akhenaten, when the name and figure of Amon were erased, but it was reconstructed in the reigns of Tutankhamon and Haremhab. In the 19th Dynasty, Ramses II carried out major work there, particularly when he constructed a new court and entrance.

In front of the **Entrance Pylon** of Ramses II, he placed six colossal statues of himself, four standing and two seated. He also erected two granite obelisks inscribed with his names and titles – one is now in the Place de la Concorde in Paris. The vertical grooves in the front section of each tower of the pylon were for the insertion of standards. The square openings above them held braces. Both towers were decorated with reliefs of Ramses' Battle of Kadesh. They are not in good condition and are somewhat difficult to see. On the right-hand tower (a) are reliefs of the Egyptian camp with Ramses II consulting with his military commanders. On the left-hand tower (b) he charges the enemy, managing to keep them engaged until reinforcements arrive.

The **Court of Ramses II** (A) is entirely surrounded by a double row of smooth-shafted papyrus columns with bud capitals. Colossi of Ramses, some usurped, stood between the columns of the first row on the rear half of the court. The shrines to the right, which were built by Hatshepsut, usurped by Thutmose III and restored by Ramses II, were dedicated to Amon (centre), Mut and Khonsu. The Fatimid Mosque of Abu el Hagag, to the left, was part of the mediaeval village built on the ruins and rubble that had accumulated in the temple.

On the right-hand rear wall of the Court is an interesting representation (at c). It shows the façade of the temple of Luxor, with one seated and two standing colossi and one obelisk on each side of the entrance gateway. The flag-staffs are in position and pennants flutter. Approaching (from the right) are some of Ramses II's sons. Behind them are fattened sacrificial animals being led by nobles. Some of the bulls have decorated horns; one has metal tips in the form of hands. Queen Nefertari is shown shaking two sistra. Behind her are princes and princesses. Ramses II had at least 111 sons and 67 daughters.

The **Colonnade** (B) was designed by Amenhotep III and decorated by Tutankhamon and Haremhab. Seti I, Ramses II and Seti II also recorded their names there. It comprises seven pairs of majestic columns, with calyx capitals. The walls are decorated with scenes of the great *Opet* festival when the sacred barges of Amon were taken in splendid procession from Karnak to Luxor temple.

This took place during the second month of the season of inundation, at the height of the flood. After twenty-four days of celebration, the barges would be returned to Karnak.

The reliefs that give a full picture of this joyous festival are in rather poor condition. The procession begins on the right-hand wall at Karnak temple, where the white-robed priests bear the sacred barge of Amon out of the gate of Karnak (d) and down to the river's edge (e). The people clap their hands in unison, acrobats perform (f); there are priestesses with sistrums (rattles), people dancing and some kneeling in adoration. The procession makes its way upstream; the king's chariot is on a boat, which is towed like the sacred barge of Amon (f). Finally, there is a sacrifice of slaughtered animals (g) and offerings to Amon, Mut and Khonsu at Luxor temple (h) with great fanfare.

On the opposite wall the return procession is shown: sacrificial bulls are led by soldiers, standard-bearers, dancers and Nubian slaves (i). The barges float downstream (j), and the final sacrifice and offerings are made to Amon and Mut at Karnak temple (k).

The **Court of Amenhotep III** (C) is a fine example of the architecture of the 18th Dynasty. The double row of columns have clustered papyrus-bud capitals and are in a good state of preservation. There were originally roofing blocks across the architraves, but the spacious central part of the court was open to the sky. The side colonnades end, in the south, with a group of columns arranged in four rows of eight, which is usually called the **Hypostyle Hall** (D). Immediately to the rear is that part of the temple that was converted into a **Roman shrine** after the removal of some columns; the doorway leading to the Sanctuary was walled into a curved recess; the reliefs were covered with plaster and painted over with the figures of Roman emperors.

Several small storerooms and priestly chambers surround the sanctuary. They are of little significance apart from what has become known as the **Birth Room** (E). Though in poor condition, the reliefs are of special interest. They depict the birth of Amenhotep III, who was not of direct royal descent, but who claimed legitimate rule due to his descent from the god Amon-Ra by miraculous birth. The story is told in relief in three rows on the left-hand wall (I):

In the bottom row (left to right) Amon converses with Thoth, god of wisdom, the pharaoh and his queen, in turn. Then he brings the Key of Life to the nostrils of the queen, and Khnum moulds two infants, representing Amenhotep and his guardian spirit or *ka* on a

Statue of Ramses II in the Great Court

potter's wheel. In the middle row (right to left), Thoth foretells the birth of her son to Amenhotep's mother. She is conducted, pregnant, to Isis and Khnum; she is seated on the birth couch, with the birth deities, Bes and Tauret beside and beneath her; to the left Amon holds the child in his arms. Beside him are Hathor and Mut. In the top row are reliefs of the suckling of the infant king and his presentation to Amon.

The inside of the **Sanctuary** (m) was rebuilt by Alexander the Great, who removed the four original columns to do so. The outer walls are decorated with reliefs that are in good condition, bearing traces of the original colour. Inside the Holy of Holies stood the gold-plated statue of the great god, which was only brought out to be viewed by the populace on special occasions like the *Opet* festival.

The Great Temple of Amon at Karnak

This great national monument of Egypt has no equal. It is not a single temple, but temple within temple, shrine within shrine, where almost all the pharaohs, particularly of the New Kingdom, wished to record their names and deeds for posterity. Though most of the structures were built in honour of Amon-Ra, his consort Mut and son Khonsu, there were numerous shrines within the complex

60

GREAT TEMPLE OF AMON AT KARNAK Plan 9

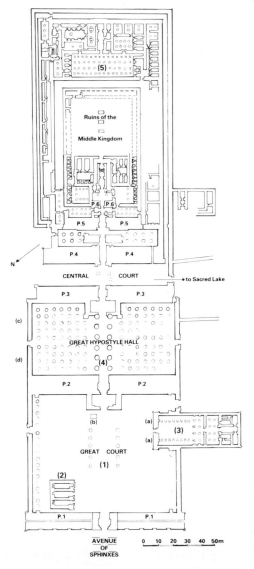

(5)

Ruins of the

Middle Kingdom

[e]

P.6 P.6

P.5   P.5

P.4   P.4

CENTRAL   COURT

→ to Sacred Lake

P.3   P.3

(c)

GREAT HYPOSTYLE HALL

(d)

(4)

P.2   P.2

(b)

(a)   **(3)**

(a)

GREAT   COURT

(1)

(2)

P.1   P.1

N

0 10 20 30 40 50m

dedicated to what might be called 'guest deities', like Ptah of Memphis and Osiris of Abydos.

As successive pharaohs replanned entrance pylons, erected colonnades and constructed temples, they often reused valuable blocks from earlier periods. In the core of the Third Pylon built by Amenhotep III, for example, there were blocks of no less than ten temples and shrines from earlier periods. In cases where it was found necessary to remove a construction completely (either for purposes of design, for political reasons, or in times of threat of war), the temple or shrine was carefully dismantled and buried.

The Sun Temples of Akhenaten suffered this fate. Thousands of distinctly uniform, decorated sandstone blocks, known as *talataat*, were buried beneath the Hypostyle Hall and the Second Pylon, as well as within the core of the Ninth and Tenth Pylons. One of the most challenging problems facing Egyptologists today is to trace the history of the temple of Amon at Karnak through such reused or buried evidence.

The **Entrance Pylon** (P. 1) was possibly constructed during the Kushite Dynasty and it was never completed. It is approached from a landing stage where there are two small obelisks erected by Seti II, down a flight of stairs, and between a double row of ram-headed sphinxes. Between the forepaws of each sphinx is a statue of Ramses II.

Entrance to Karnak is flanked by statues of rams

Hatshepsut's obelisk at Karnak (foreground) with obelisk of Thutmose I and the Hypostyle Hall

Passing through the first pylon, we enter the **Great Court** (1), which spreads over an enormous area of 8,919 square metres and contains monuments spanning many Dynasties. The single smooth-shafted column with lotus capital near the centre of the court was one of ten raised by the Kushite pharaoh Taharka. To the rear is the Second Pylon (P. 2) built at the beginning of the 19th Dynasty. To the left is a shrine (2) built by Seti II in honour of the three gods of Thebes. To the right is the Temple of Ramses III (3), which is a fine example of a traditional temple.

Temple of Ramses III (3)

This small temple, designed and built in the lifetime of a single pharaoh, is a typical New Kingdom temple. It comprises an entrance pylon with two towers flanked by statues, a central doorway leading to an open court (surrounded by colonnades), and a covered terrace to the rear. From the terrace a doorway leads to the Hypostyle Hall that is roofed; the difference in height between the central and side columns is made up by square pillars which allow light into the otherwise darkened hall. Beyond lies the Sanctuary, or Holy of Holies, where the sacred statue of the god was kept. In this temple there were three sanctuaries, for Amon, Mut and Khonsu.

In a typical temple, the pavement rises progressively and the roof lowers from the entrance to the sanctuary; this is symbolic of the primaeval hill rising from the eternal ocean. The temple also gets progressively darker, from the open court to the inner sanctuary; from the known towards the mysterious. Only the pharaoh, or the high priest in his stead, was permitted to enter the darkened sanctuary, and to cast his eyes on the statue of the god.

The inner walls of a temple were usually covered with reliefs depicting religious scenes, ritual celebrations and sacrificial offerings in honour of the gods. The outer walls were decorated with heroic scenes of war and conquest.

Ramses III recorded his victories on the entrance pylon (a). The left-hand tower shows him wearing the Double Crown. He holds a group of prisoners by the hair with one hand and raises a club to smite them with the other. Amon stands before him, handing him the Sword of Victory and delivering to him three rows of conquered cities. These are represented as a human figure rising out of a symbolic fort that bears the name of the city. On the right-hand tower the theme is repeated but with Ramses wearing the Red Crown of Lower Egypt. Two statues flank the doorway over which

Hypostyle Hall – central columns

Ramses, in relief, receives the symbol of Life from Amon.

The open court is surrounded by covered passages on three sides, each supported by eight square pillars with statues of Ramses III in the form of Osiris before each. The terrace to the rear has four square pillars and four columns with bud capitals. The reliefs on the left-hand rear wall of the pylon show Ramses receiving the hieroglyph for Jubilee from the enthroned Amon. On the right-hand wall is a procession of standard-bearers and Ramses leading the priests who bear the sacred barges of the Theban triad.

The Hypostyle Hall, which has eight columns with papyrus-bud capitals, leads to the three sanctuaries. The reliefs show Ramses making offerings before the sacred barge of each god: Amon in the central chamber, Mut to the left and Khonsu to the right.

Returning to the Great Court, we turn east and approach the **Second Pylon** (P. 2) that dates to the beginning of the 19th Dynasty. The core, as already mentioned, contained thousands of the sand-stone blocks from the Sun Temples. Also buried were discarded statues, such as the huge red granite statue of Ramses II, usurped by Pinedjem, son-in-law of the high priest of Amon. It was buried under the ruins of the northern tower and now stands to the left of the central doorway (b). A small figure of Nefertari, one of the most complete statues ever found of this beautiful queen, stands in front of his legs.

The **Great Hypostyle Hall** (4), with its 134 columns arranged in sixteen rows, covers an area of 4,983 square metres. It is the largest single chamber of any temple in the world. The double row of central columns, which lead towards the sanctuary, are higher than the side columns. Their shafts are smooth, and they soar to a height of twenty-one metres. The spreading calyx capitals retain much of their original colour, as do the massive architraves. The shorter side columns have bud capitals. The discrepancy in height is made up by square pillars between the steps of the roof that provided the only light when the hall had its original roofing.

The Hypostyle Hall was decorated throughout. All the walls and the shafts of the columns were covered with reliefs and inscriptions showing adoration of the deities, especially Amon-Ra. Seti I was responsible for the entire northern half of the hall, and Ramses II built the southern portion, but many other 19th Dynasty pharaohs recorded their names there.

On the *outside* of the Hypostyle Hall are some important historical reliefs. On the southern wall is a record of Ramses II's

KARNAK COMPLEX Plan 10

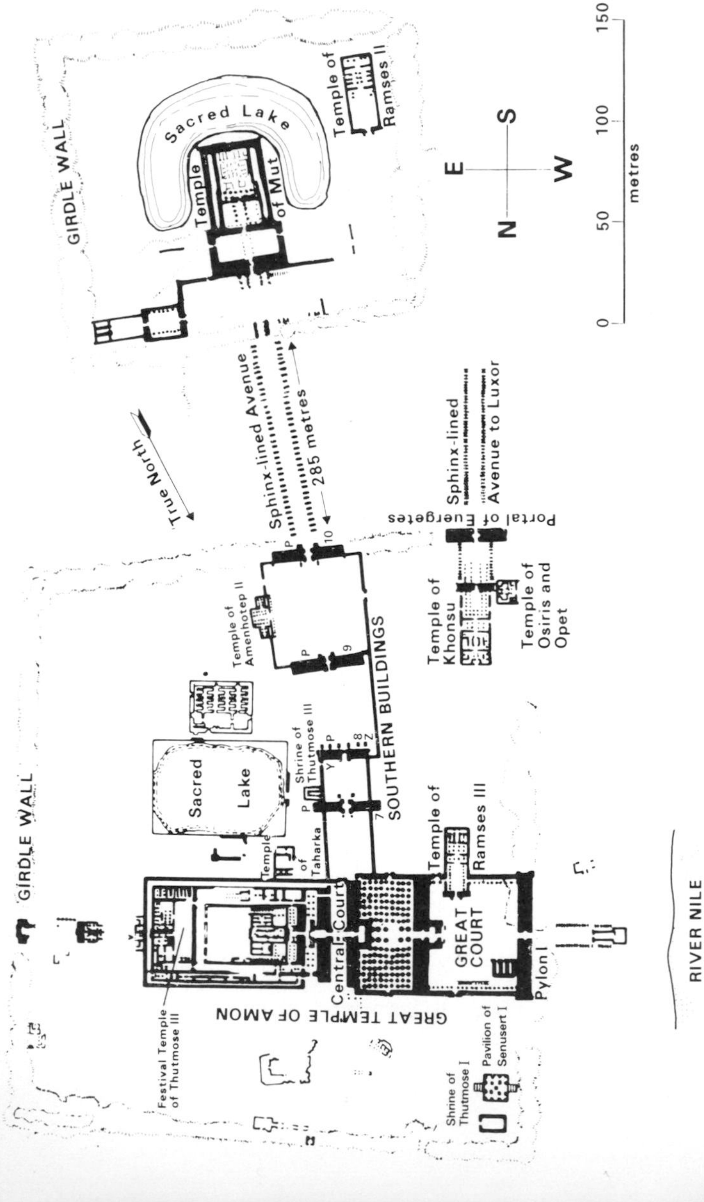

Temple of Ramses II

Sacred Lake

Temple of Mut

GIRDLE WALL

Sphinx-lined Avenue

285 metres

True North

Sphinx-lined Avenue to Luxor

Portal of Euergetes

Temple of Amenhotep II

Temple of Khonsu

Temple of Osiris and Opet

SOUTHERN BUILDINGS

Shrine of Thutmose III

Sacred Lake

Temple of Taharka

Temple of Ramses III

Central Court

GREAT COURT

Pylon I

GIRDLE WALL

Festival Temple of Thutmose III

GREAT TEMPLE OF AMON

Shrine of Thutmose I

Pavilion of Senusert I

RIVER NILE

metres

0 50 100 150

N S E W

Battle of Kadesh, which contains the actual text of the treaty with the Hittites. On the northern wall are scenes of Seti I's battles which took place in Lebanon, southern Palestine and Syria. At (c), in the upper row, we can see Seti I in his chariot shooting arrows at the enemy charioteers, cavalry and infantry who are depicted in flight. Some of the inhabitants of the conquered territory take refuge in a fortress surrounded by water. To the right Seti appears in three scenes: he binds captives, marches behind his chariot dragging four captives, and leads rows of captured Syrians to Amon, Mut and Khonsu.

In the lower row there is a triumphal march through Palestine. Seti stands in his chariot. The princes of Palestine honour him with uplifted arms while he appears to turn towards them in acknowledgement. Further along the wall is the battle against bedouin tribes in southern Palestine: some of the survivors flee to the mountains. The victorious Seti returns from Syria, along with captives. The boundary between Asia and Egypt is marked by a canal. On the Egyptian side priests and officials welcome Seti, and he delivers the captives and the booty to Amon-Ra. To the right of the doorway, at (d), are three rows of battle reliefs: the storming of Kadesh in the top row; the battle against the Libyans (with pig-tails and feathers) in the middle row; and the battle against the Hittites in northern Syria in the bottom row. On both sides of the doorway are huge reliefs of Amon-Ra who, in return for the tribute and the several rows of captured territories, which he holds by cords, presents the Sword of Victory to Seti.

The **Third Pylon** (P. 3) was built by Amenhotep III, and it once formed the entrance to the temple. During drainage operations in recent years, prior to reconstruction of the pylon, it was discovered that hundreds of blocks of earlier structures had been buried in its core. Among those that have been reconstructed are a magnificent 12th Dynasty pavilion built by Senusert I of fine-grained limestone, and an alabaster shrine of the reigns of Amenhotep I and Thutmose I.

Thutmose I ascended the throne early in the 18th Dynasty. He made the first major alterations to the original shrine of Amon-Ra built by the pharaohs of the Middle Kingdom, and also erected the first pair of obelisks at Karnak; one still stands in the Central Court between the third and fourth pylons.

Pylons P.4 and P.5, were built by Thutmose I; Hatshepsut, his daughter and builder of the famous mortuary temple of Deir el Bahri (page 72), erected another pair of huge obelisks between them.

Hatshepsut's standing obelisk, erected in the sixteenth year of her reign, was made of a single block of pink granite and rises to a height of twenty-nine and a half metres. It is one of the two tallest standing obelisks (the other is in Rome outside St John Lateran). The inscription records that it was quarried from Aswan, transported, and erected in seven months; a considerable feat in view of the fact that it weighed some 323 tons. The base of the second obelisk is still *in situ*; the upper part is near the Sacred Lake (page 70) and fragments have been taken to the museums of Boston, Liverpool, Glasgow and Sidney.

Passing through the doorway of the **Fifth Pylon** (P.5) we enter Thutmose I's second colonnade. It is now very much in ruin. Beyond rises the **sixth** and smallest **pylon** (P.6) erected by Thutmose III and restored by Seti I. On each face are lists of the tribes of Nubia, Kush and Syria, which were subjugated by Thutmose III's army. The conquered territories are, as usual, shown as an elliptical hieroglyph character surmounted by a human bust with arms bound behind the back.

Beyond the sixth pylon is the **Hall of Records**; its characteristic feature is a pair of stately granite pillars, one bearing the lotus of Upper Egypt and the other the papyrus of Lower Egypt. Together they symbolise unity between the Two Lands. This hall, constructed by Thutmose III, was where the priests of the temple kept detailed records of the sources of gifts and booty from the conquered countries. Two fine statues of the god Amon and goddess Amenet, with the features of King Tutankhamon and Queen Ankhesamon, stand to the north of the hall.

The **Sanctuary** (e) lies directly to the rear. The inner shrine is made of pink granite and carved with fine reliefs. The ceiling is adorned with stars on a black background, and the representations are of Philip Arrhidaeus, the half-brother of Alexander the Great who succeeded him to the throne, being crowned, presented to the gods and seated before an offering table.

A corridor runs around the sanctuary, enabling us to view the finely carved reliefs, particularly on the outer southern wall (to the left of the sanctuary). These are in four rows showing the pharaoh undergoing purification with water and other rituals attending his entrance into the sanctuary. There are also offering scenes and a fine representation of the sacred barge of Amon.

Great Festival Temple of Thutmose III
The **Great Festival Temple** of Thutmose III (5) lies beyond the

ruins to the east of the sanctuary. It was built in honour of Amon-Ra by the pharaoh who fought no less than seventeen battles during his reign, creating a vast empire for his country. In his thanks for victory, Thutmose III ordered the erection of this spacious and elegant temple 44 metres wide and 16 metres deep.

The roof of the temple was supported by twenty columns in two rows with unusual inverted calyx capitals – an artistic innovation that was never repeated – and thirty-two shorter, square pillars on the sides. The reliefs depict Thutmose making offerings to the gods.

Grouped around the sanctuary, which comprises three sections, were some fifty halls and chambers. One of them (to the left) has four clustered papyrus columns and unusual reliefs on the lower walls. They show different animals and exotic plants that the conqueror brought back to his country from Syria in the 25th year of his reign.

Southern Buildings (see Plan No. 10, page 66) This area is approached from the Central Court (between P.3 and P.4). The first court (6) was the site of the famous Karnak Cachette. It appears that periodically, either for political or religious reasons, or to protect them in times of threat, the priests removed objects that had been dedicated and because of their having been consecrated, buried them in sacred ground. In the Karnak Cachette thousands of objects were unearthed in 1904: stone sculptures, sphinxes and statues of

Sacred Lake at Karnak with giant scarab of Amenhotep III in the foreground

sacred animals, as well as smaller items in metal and stone. There were 47,000 bronze items alone.

The doorway to the east leads to the **Sacred Lake** (7) where the priests of Amon purified themselves and conducted religious rites. Lying on the left-hand side of the path is the upper part of the obelisk of Hatshepsut, which enables us to view the fine technique of relief carving on granite. In the sunlight it can be seen that the figure and name of Amon were chiselled out (in a scene where Hatshepsut is being crowned) and were later recarved.

The huge granite scarab, associated with the Sun-god in the form of Kheper, was dedicated to the rising sun by Amenhotep III. It was taken from his mortuary temple in the necropolis, as were many of the blocks, which were reused.

Thutmose III erected the **Seventh Pylon** (P.7), and Hatshepsut the Eighth (P.8). The **Ninth** and **Tenth Pylons** (P.9 and P.10) were built by Tutankhamon and Haremhab. As already mentioned these two latter pylons were found to be filled with *talataat* from the sun temples of Akhenaten. The word, which means 'three' in Arabic, was coined by workmen because the size of each block measured three hands' width. The total number that have been found in the Karnak complex, beneath the flag-stones of the Hypostyle Hall, in the Second Pylon, and in the Ninth and Tenth Pylons, numbers over 40,000.

It would appear that the sun temples were built before Akhenaten transferred the capital to Tel el Amarna (Chapter 4). After his death, however, and with the reinstatement of the priests of Amon, the temples were dismantled and the blocks re-used and hidden from sight. (Some three hundred blocks have been reconstructed in an 18-metre wall in the Luxor Museum.)

The eastern avenue of sphinxes extends from the 10th Pylon to the **Temple of Mut**, consort of Amon, which is now being excavated and reconstructed. To the west of the Southern Buildings are the temple of Khonsu (8) and the adjoining temple of Osiris and Opet (9), which was built in the Ptolemaic Period.

The Temple of Khonsu

The Temple of Khonsu (8) was started by Ramses III, and like his small temple in the Great Court, it is a classical New Kingdom temple. It was dedicated to the moon-god Khonsu, son of the Theban triad. The reliefs were completed by Ramses IV, Ramses XII and Hrihor, the high priest who usurped the throne at the end of the 20th Dynasty.

The entrance pylon bears representations of Hrihor and his wife making sacrifices to the Theban deities. He stands in the position and posture traditionally assumed by the pharaohs of Egypt. The temple is, therefore, of historical importance, bearing witness to the transmission of pharaonic power from the royal line to the priests of Amon, around 1080 BC. In this temple the name of a high priest appears in a royal *cartouche* for the first time.

The ceremonial gate (southern gate) was built by Ptolemy III Euergetes (222 BC). Between it and Luxor Temple to the south were the palaces, villas, factories and markets of the inhabitants of ancient Thebes, now lost beneath the accumulated ruins of successive generations who have inhabited the same place. There was also a sphinx-lined avenue along which ceremonial processions travelled between the two temples.

THE NECROPOLIS

The necropolis lies on the western bank of the Nile at Luxor. Its monuments include a series of mortuary temples built by the pharaohs of the New Kingdom, royal tombs in the Valley of the Kings and the Valley of the Queens, and hundreds of tombs of noblemen that extend from the Dra Abu el Naga in the north to the Asasif in the south.

Although it is known as the 'city of the dead', the necropolis was once a populated and busy community. Beside each mortuary temple there were dwellings for the different orders of priests, stalls for sacrificial animals, guard-houses and store-houses, each with its superintendent. Surrounding, or in front of each temple there were lakes, groves and beautifully laid out gardens; some of the plants were imported from Syria and Punt.

The pharaohs themselves took up temporary residence on the necropolis to watch the progress being made on their mortuary temples, and supervise their construction and decoration. Excavations at Kurna, the Ramesseum and Medinet Habu have revealed large palaces with numerous chambers. The largest and best preserved of these complexes lies to the south of Medinet Habu, where Ramses III watched his name being carved, literally, in history.

Also on the necropolis, at Deir el Medina, was a village of workers who carried out the secret task of digging and decorating the royal tombs in the Valley of the Kings. Excavations over the last half century have revealed that this walled city contained some eighty families. Their professions ranged from quarrying and mortar-mixing, to draughting, painting and designing. There were scribes and foremen, and a director of works who headed the community. Each family had a simple, sparsely furnished house, and they constructed the tombs nearby. From the tombs at Deir el Medina, and from some 40,000 pieces of inscribed pottery (ostraka) found at the site, archaeologists have been able to trace the activities of this community for generation upon generation, throughout a span of nearly three centuries. Their very personalities have been revealed: pride in their professional activities, joy at family celebrations, and even their grievances.

MORTUARY TEMPLES

The Colossus of Memnon and its companion
These two somewhat weathered seated statues greet visitors to the necropolis. They are all that remain of what was once the largest mortuary temple in the necropolis, that of Amenhotep III. It is somewhat difficult, today, to imagine a temple which, with its gardens and lake, extended from the Ramesseum to Medinet Habu.

Amenhotep's mortuary temple was probably badly damaged from a high flood. Since then time and neglect wrought havoc with it. In the 19th Dynasty, Ramses II's son Merenptah used some of the fallen blocks for his own, neighbouring, temple. Finally, nothing was left but these two lonely sentinels on the plain, and, a quarter of a mile away to the rear, a huge sandstone stelae weighing some 150 tons, referring to the dedication of the temple.

When an earthquake caused the upper part of the northern statue to fall down, cracks and holes appeared in it. At dawn, when the breeze blew through these, it created a musical sound, which the Greeks and Romans explained in their mythology: when Memnon fell at Troy he reappeared at Thebes as a singing stone statue. At sunrise he would greet his mother Aurora with a plaintive song. Aurora, on hearing the sound, shed tears in the form of the morning dew on the cold stone of the statue. When the cracks were filled in during the reign of Septimius Severus, AD 193, the sound was no longer heard.

The Mortuary Temple of Hatshepsut (Deir el Bahri)
The mortuary temple of Hatshepsut is the most beautiful in the necropolis, and the queen herself is one of the most colourful figures in ancient Egyptian history. She was the daughter of Thutmose I

Colossi of Memnon

and the only one of his children of direct royal lineage, being the child of the Great Royal Wife, Queen Ahmose. Her two half-brothers were by lesser wives. However, Hatshepsut ruled concurrently with Thutmose II and his son, Thutmose III.

For half a century (*c*. 1500–1450 BC) there occurred what is usually regarded as a feud in the family of the Thutmosides: evidence of pharaonic vanity (Hatshepsut removed part of the roof of her father's colonnade at Karnak in order to erect her great granite obelisks), petty jealousy (Thutmose III later built a wall to hide her obelisks and removed her name in order to insert his own), and what might be seen as vicious acts of frustration. Hatshepsut's body has never been identified with certainty. Her red sandstone sarcophagus had been enlarged to receive the body of her father, Thutmose I, while her own sarcophagus contained the mummy of Thutmose II, who appears to have died prematurely, after a short co-regency with Hatshepsut. Then, when Thutmose III finally came to the throne, he obliterated all references to the 'female pharaoh' from every temple in the land, particularly from Deir el Bahri.

Hatsheptsut is also a romantic figure, for her name is closely linked with that of her architect, Senmut, who designed her terraced sanctuary. He rose from the position of tutor to her daughter to one

MORTUARY TEMPLE OF HATSHEPSUT Plan 11

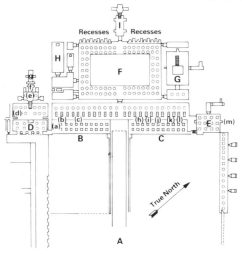

of great influence in the court. In fact, he was granted the privilege of constructing his tomb below the mortuary temple of his queen, and inscriptions in some parts of her temple show that they were intimately related.

Hatshepsut, as pharaoh, wore a royal kilt and the ceremonial beard, which were symbols of kingship. Her temple was designed, like the adjacent 11th Dynasty mortuary temple of Mentuhotep the Great, with terraced courts. These rose, one above the other, by connecting inclined planes at the centre. Ascending from the **Lower Court** we pass through two colonnades. The reliefs to the south show the transportation of two obelisks by river. In one register they can be seen on the deck of a barge, and in the other a trumpeter leads a group of archers to the inauguration ceremony.

The **Central Court** (A) was where Hatshepsut planted the incense trees that were imported in small tubs from the Land of Punt. The whole story is related in relief in the famed Punt Colonnade to the left. The corresponding colonnade to the right is the Birth Colonnade that records Hatshepsut's divine birth.

The **Punt Colonnade** (B) commemorates the expedition that Hatshepsut made to Punt, on the Somali coast, under the orders of Amon. On the left-hand wall (a) is the village of Punt. The houses are constructed on stilts, with ladders leading to the entrances. The inhabitants of Punt greet the Egyptian envoy and his officials, and show them products for barter. The fat, ungainly Queen of Punt is there, along with the donkey on which she travelled. With their inherent wit, the ancient Egyptians inscribed a text near the donkey reading: 'This is the donkey that carried his wife'.

A scene of the Egyptian fleet setting sail, and arriving in Punt can be seen on the rear wall (b). The incense trees are transported aboard the vessel in tubs. At the centre of the wall (c), Hatshepsut (defaced) offers the fruits of her expedition to Amon: incense trees, wild game, cattle, electrum and bows.

The **Shrine of Hathor** (D) lies to the left of the Punt Colonnade. It has two roofed-in colonnades that are supported by Hathor columns, leading to the shrine, which comprises three chambers, one behind the other. The second colonnade has some interesting reliefs. On the right-hand wall Thutmose III, holding an oar, stands in the presence of different deities. There are rows of ships with canopies and thrones. It is a festal scene with soldiers and fan-bearers. On the rear wall is a representation of Thutmose III (replacing Hatshepsut) having his hand licked by the Hathor cow. And, on the left-hand wall (d) is a boat containing the Hathor cow with the monarch drinking from the udder.

In the first chamber of the shrine (e) Hatshepsut (or Thutmose III) is represented with the deities. The colour, especially on the ceiling, is excellent. The second chamber (f) has a fine relief of Hatshepsut (scraped) making offerings to Hathor, who stands on the sacred barge beneath a canopy. A little nude boy holds a sistrum in front of the erased figure of the queen. The third chamber (g) has an unusual pointed roof, and the wall reliefs show Hatshepsut (on each of the side walls) drinking from the udder of the cow, Hathor, with Amon standing before them. On the rear wall the queen stands before Hathor and Amon, with the latter holding the hieroglyph for Life (*Ankh*) to her face.

The **Birth Colonnade** (C) is adorned with a series of reliefs 'proving' Hatshepsut's right to the throne by divine birth. On the rear wall (h) is a scene showing a council of gods in the presence of Amon. Then Thoth, god of wisdom, leads Amon (figure erased), to the bedchamber of Queen Ahmose (i). The seated Amon faces the queen and impregnates her with the *Ankh*, the breath of life, held to her nostrils. Near the centre of the wall (j) the queen mother is large with child. She stands, dignified in her pregnancy, smiling with contentment as she is led to the birth room.

The scene in which Amon and the queen mother are borne to the heavens by two goddesses (k) is badly damaged. In the scene of the actual birth (also badly damaged), the queen mother sits on a chair that is placed on a sort of lion-headed bed held aloft by various gods (l). The scene of Hatshepsut and her *ka* being fashioned on a potter's wheel by the ram-headed god Khnum has also been erased, but in the scene towards the end of the wall they pass through the hands of various goddesses who record the divine birth. Witnesses are the ibis-headed Thoth, the ram-headed Khnum and the frog-headed Heket.

To the right of the Birth Colonnade is the well-preserved **Shrine of Anubis** (E). On the right-hand wall (m) – above a small recess – is a scene of the queen (damaged) making a wine-offering to the hawk-headed Sokar, a god of the dead. On the rear wall offerings are made to Amon (to the left) and Anubis (to the right) with the sacrificial gifts heaped up before each.

The **Upper Court** (F) is being reconstructed and is closed to visitors. In the open-roofed chamber to the right (G) is an ancient altar for the cult of Ra, the Sun-god. To the left (H) is a sacrificial hall. The **Sanctuary** (I) is hewn out of the natural rock, and comprises two chambers with large recesses to the sides. The innermost chamber was hollowed out of the mountain in Ptolemaic times, and was dedicated to the cults of two of Egypt's wise men: Imhotep, the builder of Zoser's Step Pyramid at Sakkara (2686 BC) and Amenhotep, son of Hapu, the architect who lived in the reign of Amenhotep III (1390 BC). Both these wise men were worshipped as gods of healing in Ptolemaic times, and it would seem that Hatshepsut, builder of the mortuary temple, had been forgotten. The Ptolemies regarded the building as a mystical sanctuary connected with these two wise men and, in fact, Deir el Bahri came to be regarded as a place of healing. In the Christian era the upper terrace was converted into a monastery, which gave the temple its name: Deir (monastery) el Bahri (the northern).

Mortuary Temple of Seti I (Kurna)

This temple was built by Seti I in reverent memory of his father, Ramses I, who ruled for little more than a year, and, of course, for his own cult. It was completed by his son, Ramses II. Only the rear part of the temple survives, but it contains some of the finest relief work in the Nile valley. Seti I started an art and architectural revival during his reign. He wished to return to the traditional canons of Egyptian art after the so-called Amarna period, and his two temples, at Kurna and Abydos (page 21), have delicate, classical reliefs.

MORTUARY TEMPLE OF SETI I (KURNA) Plan 12

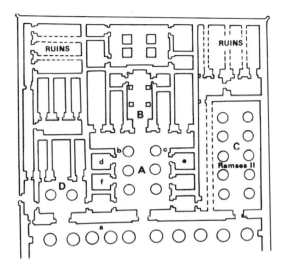

The first court was totally destroyed, and a row of columns are all that remain of the colonnade of the second court. To the left and right of the central doorway are figures of men and women alternately. Those to the south (a) have lotuses on their heads, representing Upper Egypt; the figures to the north have papyri, representing Lower Egypt. All bear flowers, cakes and caskets.

The **Hypostyle Hall** (A) is flanked by small chambers on each side. The walls between them have reliefs of Seti I and Ramses II with the various deities. At (b) and (c) Seti is nourished by Mut, wife of Amon-Ra, and Hathor, respectively.

The fine-textured limestone of this temple was worked with flair and precision. The reliefs of the side chambers are beautifully carved. In (d) is a scene of the enthroned Seti between Amon-Ra and his consort Mut on one side, and Ptah and his consort Sekhmet, on the other. In (e) Seti makes offerings to Osiris; Isis, Hathor and Nephthys stand behind the throne. In (f) the enthroned, deified, Seti receives offerings from other gods; they include Wepwawat, the wolf-jackal of Abydos.

In the **Sanctuary** (B) there are four simple square pillars and the base of the sacred barge. The reliefs show Seti making offerings.

78

MORTUARY TEMPLE OF RAMSES II
(RAMESSEUM) Plan 13

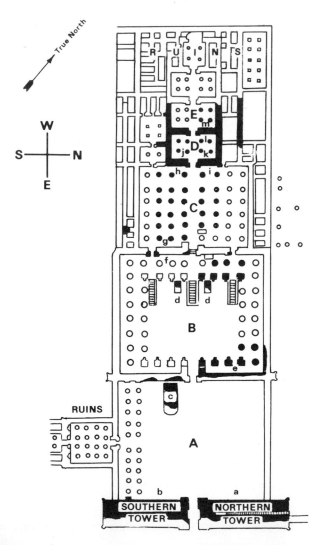

(Seti I's battles against the Libyans, Hittites and Syrians, would have been depicted on the pylons, which have been destroyed.)

Mortuary Temple of Ramses II (The Ramesseum)

Ramses II left a greater mark in history than many other accomplished and successful pharaohs, such as Ahmose (who won the war of liberation against the Hyksos) and Thutmose III (who won a great empire). The reason is that Ramses II had one of the longest reigns in Egyptian history. He ruled for 67 years and built more numerous monuments, of greater size, than any other pharaoh. He repeated, in huge and detailed relief, his victory during the Battle of Kadesh in the 5th year of his reign.

The history of the battle may be summarised as follows: Ramses II's objective was to capture the Hittite stronghold of Kadesh on the Orontes river in Syria. He encountered little resistance until he approached the north-west of Kadesh, when his intelligence brought two prisoners of war (who were, in fact, spies). They told Ramses that the Hittite King Muwatallish had retreated in fear of the advancing Egyptian army, and Ramses II was delighted to hear this.

Without taking even the most elementary precautions, he pitched camp, making ready for his march on Kadesh the next day. But the Hittite army lay hidden beyond the crest of a hill. They took Ramses completely by surprise and, in fact, his first brigade was completely cut off from the rest of his forces. It was fortunate for Ramses that the Hittite army was not as well organised as the Egyptian. After several chariot charges, and the timely arrival of his other battalions, the tables were turned, and Ramses drove the enemy back. Although, he did not achieve his objective, Kadesh, neither did he suffer a defeat.

A poem was written about Ramses II's military prowess by an unknown poet, who lauded his bravery and victory. He liked it so much that he had it inscribed on his monuments of which there were many; from Nubia to the Mediterranean he was honoured as hero.

Ramses II suppressed some Nubian revolts during his reign, and also carried out a campaign in Libya. His greatest accomplishment however, is the one about which least is known; his protection of Egypt from a threat from the sea. Recent excavations along the Mediterranean coast have revealed a series of fortresses which he built, and which achieved their purpose. The battles against the 'People of the Sea', only occurred some thirty years after Ramses II's death, in the reign of his successor, Ramses III.

Both towers of the **Entrance Pylon** are badly damaged. The inside of the northern tower (a) has scenes of the Egyptian camp and the southern tower (b) scenes of the battle.

Towards the south-eastern corner of the **First Court** (A) lie the remains of what was once the biggest colossus of the pharaoh (c) and, without doubt, one of the most enormous pieces of stone ever fashioned. The remains of this perfectly sculpted and polished granite statue include the chest, upper arm and foot. Careful measurements have been made and it is estimated that the statue's total height must have been over seventeen metres, and its weight over a thousand tons. It was transported from the quarries of Aswan in one piece.

The **Second Court** (B) had colonnades on all four sides and a terrace to the rear. On each side of the central stairway leading to the terrace were monoliths of the king (d). Facing the court were still more statues of Ramses II backed by Osiride pillars. The representations on the shafts of the columns show him sacrificing to the deities.

To the right of the doorway (e), are more scenes of the Battle of Kadesh (lower registers) with Ramses in his chariot, and the enemy pierced by arrows or trampled beneath the horse's hooves. In the upper registers are reliefs of the Festival of the god Min. This important festival was celebrated at the time of the harvest. The priests, who stand to the side of the pharaoh, await a procession headed by other priests. They carry images of the royal ancestors. Four birds are released, to carry the royal tidings to the four corners of the earth. Ramses cuts a sheaf with a sickle to present to the god Min.

The terrace to the rear is approached by a stairway. On the left-hand wall (f) there are well-preserved reliefs showing Ramses II (to the right), kneeling before Amon, Mut and Khonsu. Thoth, who is behind him, records his name for eternal remembrance. To the left, the hawk-headed Montu holds the hieroglyph for life before the king's face; and Atum leads him forward. The scenes of the top register show offerings to the deities, and those on the bottom depict Ramses as a family man with many of his sons.

The **Hypostyle Hall** (C) is similar to that of Karnak; it also has taller columns at the centre with spreading calyx-capitals, and lower ones at the sides with bud capitals. The difference in height is made up of pillars with the spaces creating windows which afford light into the hall. All the reliefs show Ramses II in battle. He storms the fortress, at (g), and is shown in vigorous battle. His sons took part and proved themselves worthy of their heroic father. Each is identifiable by his name engraved beside him, at (h) and (i).

Beyond the Hypostyle Hall are two smaller halls, one behind the other. The first (D) has astrological representations on the roof, and scenes of priests bearing the sacred boats of Amon, Mut and Khonsu (j) and (k). On the rear right-hand wall (l) Ramses is seated beneath the sacred persea tree of Heliopolis, on the leaves of which his names are being written by the god Atum, the goddess Sheshat, and Thoth.

The second hall (E) is mostly in ruin. It has some sacrificial representations that include a scene of Ramses burning incense to Ptah and Sekhmet (m).

The mortuary temple was surrounded by store-rooms and priestly chambers and, as already mentioned, there was a palace complex to the south where Ramses watched the work being executed.

MEDINET HABU

Second Court of Medinet Habu

Medinet Habu is the name given to a large group of buildings that were started in the 18th Dynasty, but on which construction continued through to Roman times. The main feature of the

82

MORTUARY TEMPLE OF RAMSES III (MEDINET HABU) Plan 14

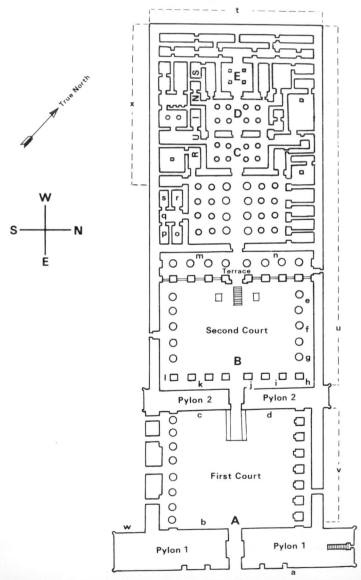

complex is the mortuary temple of Ramses III. It is approached by passing through an unusual entrance structure which he built. It is known as the Pavillion, and was undoubtedly inspired by Syrian fortresses (*migdols*). In front of it are two small watch-towers and a battlement of elevated stonework. It has two upper storeys containing several small apartments with scenes of the pharaoh and his wives.

Passing through the entrance we cross a large court. There are ruins of a temple built by Hatshepsut to the right, and a 25th Dynasty shrine to the left. Further back is the main temple.

THE MORTUARY TEMPLE OF RAMSES III

Ramses III ruled Egypt for some thirty years during the 20th Dynasty, when central power was weakening, foreign influence was declining and internal security was poor. In fact, he was the last Ramses of any consequence. After his death the state priesthood of Amon acquired increasing power and finally seized the throne and overthrew the Dynasty.

Ramses III had successful battles in Asia and in Nubia. His most important battle was against the 'People of the Sea' who attacked Egypt's Mediterranean coast. This battle, and his wars in neighbouring lands, were recorded in his temple. It was built on the same plan as the Ramesseum of Ramses II, but is unique in having been contructed and decorated progressively, as the campaigns of Ramses III occurred. It therefore provides a step-by-step record of his military career, and has the added advantage of being extremely well preserved.

The **First Pylon** is covered on both sides with representations and inscriptions of Ramses III's military triumphs. On both towers there are grooves for flag-staffs, and the pharaoh is depicted in the traditional pose of dangling enemies by the hair while he smites them with his club. On the northern tower (a) he wears the Red Crown and stands before Ra-Harakhte. On the southern tower he wears the White Crown and smites the captives before Amon-Ra. Both gods lead forward groups of captives. The captured lands are shown as circular forts inscribed with the names of the cities and surmounted by bound captives.

At the foot of the pylons the scenes show Amon seated, with Ptah standing behind him, inscribing the pharaoh's name on a palm leaf; the pharaoh kneeling before Amon and receiving the hieroglyph for 'Jubilee of the Reign' suspended on a palm-branch, and Thoth writing the king's name on the leaves of the tree.

The **First Court** (A) had a colonnade with calyx capitals to the left, and Osirid figures to the right; the latter were badly ruined by the early Christians. There is an interesting representation on the inner side of the first pylon (b). This is the Libyan campaign in which mercenaries took part. They are recognisable by the round helmets on their heads, ornamented with horns. The pharaoh, in his chariot, charges the enemy and overthrows them. The scenes on the side walls repeat the victorious war themes, and the triumphant return of the king with his captives to attend the great Feast of Amon.

To the rear of the court, at (c), Ramses leads three rows of prisoners to Amon and Mut. They wear caps adorned with feathers and aprons decorated with tassles. At (d) there is a long series of inscriptions recording Ramses' military triumph over the 'Great League of Sea Peoples'.

An inclined plane leads us through the granite gateway of the Second Pylon and into the **Second Court** (B), which was later converted into a church. Due to covering the 'heathen' representations with clay, the reliefs have been preserved in good condition. On both sides of the court are marvellous processional scenes. Those on the right represent the Great Festival of the God Min, and those to the left, the Festival Ptah–Sokaris. The scenes in honour of Min, like those of the Ramesseum, show trumpeters, drummers and castanet-players. In one scene the pharaoh is borne on a richly-decorated carrying chair with a canopy (e). He is led by priests and soldiers, and followed by his courtiers. He sacrifices to Min (f) and, in the sacred procession, marches behind the white bull, the sacred animal of Min (g) and (h). Priests, the queen, and a procession of priests in two rows carry standards and images of the pharaoh and his ancestors. Like his predecessor, Ramses II, Ramses III watches the priests allow four birds to fly to the four corners of the earth to carry the royal tidings. Also, he cuts a sheaf of wheat with his sickle in the presence of priests and his queen (i), and he offers incense to Min (j). The scenes from the Festival of Ptah–Sokaris to the left of the court are depicted in the upper registers.

There are some interesting war reliefs, which start at the inner wall of the second pylon (k). The first scene shows Ramses III attacking the Libyans with his charioteers. He shoots arrows with his bow and the infantry flee in all directions. The mercenaries are in the lower row. The second scene shows him returning from battle with three rows of fettered Libyans tied before him, and two fan-bearers behind. The third shows him leading his prisoners of war to Amon and Mut.

In the corner (l) Ramses turns in his chariot to receive four rows of prisoners of war from noblemen; among them are his own sons. Hands and phalluses of the slain are counted. On the lower reaches of the rear walls of the terrace (m) and (n) are rows of royal princes and princesses.

The **Great Hypostyle Hall** follows. The roof was originally supported by twenty-four columns in four rows of six, with the double row of central columns thicker than the others. The wall reliefs show Ramses in the presence of the various deities. Adjoining each side of the hall are a series of chambers. Those to the left (o) to (r), stored valuable jewels, musical instruments, costly vessels and precious metals, including gold.

There are two small hypostyle halls (C) and (D), to the rear, each supported by eight columns, leading to the sanctuary (E). In the second of the hypostyle halls (D) there are granite dyads, or statues of Ramses II with a deity, he is shown seated with the ibis headed Thoth, to the right, and with Maat, goddess of Truth, to the left.

On the *outside* of the temple there are important historical reliefs that commemorate the wars of Ramses III. Those to the rear of the temple (t) show the pharaoh's battle against the Nubians: the actual battle scene is shown, also the triumphal procession with captives, and the presentation to Amon. On the northern wall (u) are ten scenes from the wars against the Libyans, and the naval victory over the 'People of the Sea'. The latter is an extremely animated representation: Ramses alights from his chariot and shoots at the hostile fleet. One enemy ship has capsized, and the Egyptian vessels (distinguishable by a lion's head on the prow) are steered by men with large oars, while the rest of the crew row from benches. Bound captives are inside the hold.

The northern wall, at (v) has scenes from the Syrian wars, which include the storming of a fortress, and the presentation of prisoners to Amon and Khonsu. On the back of the first pylon (w) is a hunt for deer, bulls and asses in the marshes. On the southern wall, at (x) is a Festival Calendar that includes a list of appointed sacrifices, as dating from the accession of Ramses III to the throne.

VALLEY OF THE KINGS

Deep in the limestone hills to the north-west of Deir el Bahri is a remote valley. Here the pharaohs of the 18th, 19th and 20th

Dynasties chose their eternal resting place. Thutmose I was the first pharaoh to excavate a tomb in the barren valley, and to construct his mortuary temple at the edge of the verdant valley. In this way, he believed, his cult could be continued while his resting place remained secret and safe from robbers.

After the mummified bodies of the pharaohs had been laid to rest, the passages were sealed and covered with rock and rubble. With the entrances totally obscured, the New Kingdom pharaohs were confident that their tombs, unlike those of their ancestors, would be safe. They were mistaken. With the notable exception of the burial of Tutankhamon all were broken into and robbed of their treasures. The huge stone lids of the sarcophagi were thrust aside, or hammered off. The inner coffins were removed. The mummies of the pharaohs were stripped of their adornments and cast aside, sometimes actually burnt, by the robbers.

In an attempt to protect the bodies of their great ancestors, the priests of the 21st Dynasty placed them in a twelve-metre deep shaft, which was probably a Middle Kingdom tomb, in one of the caves at the foot of the cliffs at Deir el Bahri; that is to say, on the other side of the mountain that separates the Valley of the Kings from Deir el Bahri. Into this shaft they placed no less than forty mummies of the 18th and 19th Dynasties, which they had collected from pillaged tombs. The bodies of Amenhotep I, Thutmose III, Seti I, Ramses II and Ramses III were among them. Other mummies were hidden in already violated tombs, such as that of Amenhotep II (page 91), which was then resealed.

The shaft at Deir el Bahri was discovered in 1881, and the mummies in the tomb of Amenhotep II in 1898. All were taken from one place to another, until they were settled on the upper floor of the Cairo Museum of Antiquities.

Tomb design and decoration

The actual tomb design was relatively uniform, differing only in length and number of chambers. They usually comprised three corridors, one following the other, sloping deeper and deeper into the bedrock. A shaft at the end of the first corridor, sometimes dropping to a depth of over six metres, was a feature of several tombs; perhaps it was designed to discourage robbers who, despite all effort at concealment, had located the doorway, or for drainage of rainfall. At the end of the third corridor there was usually a door leading to an ante-chamber, and the tomb chamber lay beyond this. Its roof was often supported by pillars and the sarcophagus was placed either at the centre or to the rear.

Mortuary Literature

In most of the royal tombs from the entrance doorway to the burial chamber, the walls from floor to ceiling were covered with sacred texts and representations from the mortuary literature known as the **Book of the Dead**. This had been accumulated over thousands of years and included hymns, prayers and magical utterances, as well as ascension texts and resurrection texts. The corridors represented the different stages of the journey of the deceased to the afterlife.

The ancient Egyptians had a deeply rooted concept of life after death. They saw the physical body as a vehicle for certain immortal aspects of man that continued after his death. One of these was known as the *ka* (symbolised as a pair of upraised arms), which was a sort of guardian spirit that was born at the same time as man, and continued to live in the vicinity of his tomb after his death. Another immortal aspect was the *ba* or soul, symbolised as a bird with a human head which came into existence with the passing of the mortal body. All the mortuary literature in ancient Egypt listed provisions of food and offerings to nourish the *ka* and prayers for the release of the *ba*.

The pharaoh was regarded as 'Son of the Sun-god'. This led to the belief that at his death he would join, or be absorbed by, the sun when it set on the western horizon. He would travel through the twelve regions of the underworld (which correspond to the twelve hours of night) in the solar barge. Sometimes the vessel would be piloted by the wolf jackal of Abydos, who steered it through the underworld, or along the horizon. Then, just as the sun would rise again in the eastern sky, so, too, would the pharaoh be reborn.

In the early corridors of the tomb there were selections from 'The Praises of Ra', often with the Sun-god depicted in many different forms. This was followed by the 'Book of the Portals', which was an hour-by-hour division of the underworld, each separated by a massive gate guarded by gigantic serpents. With the correct password, however, and the necessary protection from guardian deities and sacred charms, the deceased would successfully pass from one hour to another. The banks of the river would usually throng with spirits and demons of a friendly nature to ward off the many enemies of the Sun-god, whose purpose was to hinder the journey of the solar barge.

The mortuary texts known as 'The sun's journey in the Underworld' revealed a land where ferocious, dragon-like creatures, serpents and crocodiles lurked. Among the deadly foes of the deceased, some would deprive him of his mortuary food and drink, dry up his breath, or cause him to breathe fire. They could rob him of his organs and, worse, his very name, which would deprive him of his identity forever.

In the deepest chambers of the tomb monsters and spirits can often be seen in rows. To each the deceased addressed an appropriate speech. The priests ingeniously devised a choice of Two Ways, so that if the deceased deviated from the correct path, there were charms to save him from the 'Place of the Execution by the Gods', to prevent him being overpowered by the forces of evil, to prevent him from becoming 'The blazing Eye of Horus', and to prevent him from walking with his head downwards! The list was endless. There were safeguards for every stage of the journey, even a special scarab over the heart, to quieten its beat in the awesome presence of Osiris, Lord of the Underworld.

Osiris, Lord of the Underworld

The concept of a court in the underworld only fully developed in the Middle Kingdom, when it was believed that the deceased would stand before Osiris, as final judge, and answer charges. With Osiris were his devoted wife Isis, her sister Nephthys, Thoth, the god of Wisdom, and forty-two judges of the dead. Before this impressive court, the deceased would swear innocence by what is known as the 'negative confession'. He would declare that he had not stolen food, spoken evil or falsehood, robbed the dead, harmed anyone, or slain a sacred animal; nor was he arrogant, fraudulent or blasphemous, etc.

Osiris was usually depicted seated beneath a canopy in mummified form, as befitted a legendary ancestor. His face was green (the colour of the rebirth of the land) or dark (like a mummy), as befitted a legendary ancestor. On his head was the tall white crown. In his hands were his sacred emblems, the crook and the flail.

The tomb of Haremhab shows that after completion of the negative confession, the ibis-headed Thoth watched over the weighing of the heart of the deceased against Maat, the feather of truth, and recorded the verdict. Those who failed were condemned to eternal darkness, hunger and thirst, or were hurled to a ferocious animal the 'eater of hearts'. Those who led a blameless life gained access to the afterlife; this was sometimes believed to lie west of Abydos, and sometimes conceived of as among the 'Shining Ones' in heaven.

Tomb of Thutmose III (34)

This is the tomb of the pharaoh who won an empire for his country, and who built a great Festival Temple at Karnak in thanksgiving to Amon-Ra for victory. He chose a remote site in the Valley of the Kings for his tomb. It is approached up a steep ladder that is located at the end of a narrow, rocky ravine. The entrance is high up in the cliff face. From there a sloping corridor leads to a staircase (1) that is flanked by broad niches, another corridor that has a deep pit (now bridged), and two chambers.

The first chamber (2) is of irregular shape. The ceiling, decorated with stars, is supported by two undecorated pillars, and the walls bear the names of 476 different deities and demons of the underworld.

The main chamber (3), approached by another stairway, is oval; deliberately cut reminiscent of the shape of the cartouche, and is flanked by side chambers. The mortuary texts on the walls are simple line drawings and citations of the divisions of the underworld. The first of the two pillars is particularly noteworthy. On one face Thutmose III is shown in three registers. At the top he is depicted in a boat with the queen mother, whose name was Isis. She seems to have been of no particular importance, but her son wished to immortalise her by depicting her in his tomb. In the second register he is shown being suckled by the sacred tree that is usually

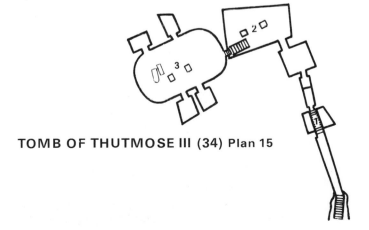

TOMB OF THUTMOSE III (34) Plan 15

Tomb of Amenhotep II; Amenhotep with Osiris

associated with the goddess Nut, but is here associated with the goddess Isis. In the third register Thutmose is followed by several female members of the royal family.

Despite the remoteness of the tomb, and all the precautions taken to safeguard it from tomb robbers, it was robbed in ancient times. The mummy of the pharaoh was left in it and later removed by the priests to the shaft at Deir el Bahri. The red sandstone sarcophagus remains in the main chamber with the overthrown lid beside it.

Tomb of Amenhotep II (35)
Amenhotep's tomb is one of the most beautiful in the Valley of the Kings. When it was excavated in 1898 it was found to contain, not only the mummy of Amenhotep himself, festooned and garlanded, but other mummified bodies as well, including nine of royalty.

Apparently the tomb had been violated in ancient times and robbed of all its treasures, with the exception of the quartzite-sandstone sarcophagus. The priests, who reasoned that the robbers would not return to the tomb, decided to bury there the bodies saved from other tombs. This last attempt to safeguard the mummies was successful. Among those identified were the mummies of Thutmose IV, Amenhotep III, Seti II, Ramses IV, V and VI.

The first corridors of Amenhotep's tomb are rough and un-decorated. They lead to a pit (now bridged), a false burial chamber (1) and finally the tomb chamber (2). The tomb chamber is supported by six pillars decorated with figures of the dead pharaoh and the great gods. The outlines are in black. The crowns, jewellery, belts and border decorations are in colour. They are offset by the dark blue roof, covered with stars.

TOMB OF AMENHOTEP II (35)

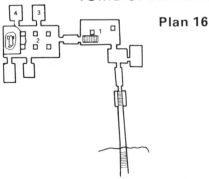

Plan 16

The walls are painted terracotta and the mortuary texts are so drawn that they give the impression of papyrus texts pinned to the walls. There is not too much detail or use of colour and the effect is austere and dignified.

On each side of the tomb chamber are two rooms. Three mummies lay in the first to the right (3) and the nine royal mummies in the second (4). One of the mummies proved to be that of Queen Tiy; her hair was scientifically compared with that found in a symbolic coffin in the tomb of Tutankhamon, and found to be of the same type.

Tomb of Tutankhamon (62)

This famous tomb is amongst the smallest in the Valley of the Kings. Nevertheless it contained treasures which may have represented the most abundant hoard ever buried in the valley. For, contrary to initial belief that the treasure belonged to a boy-king who had a short and not very significant reign, it is now known that some of the objects date back not only to the Amarna period, but even to the reign of Thutmose III. The five thousand-odd objects catalogued from the tomb, therefore, represent a uniquely accumulated collection and, perhaps, the richest placed in any tomb.

The first chamber (A), which measures a mere 8×4 metres, is undecorated. Bare, too, are the walls of the small Annex (B). The

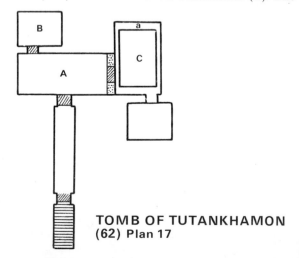

TOMB OF TUTANKHAMON (62) Plan 17

only chamber with decorated walls is the burial chamber itself (C).

The burial chamber was originally sealed off by a plastered wall, before which stood two life-sized statues of Tutankhamon in dark varnished wood, with gold ornaments, headdress and kilt. When the wall was broken through, the outermost shrine of wood, covered with gold-leaf, was revealed. Within it were three similar, smaller shrines, one inside the other. The sarcophagus of crystalline sandstone lay at the centre.

Inside the sarcophagus were two wooden coffins in portrait images of the king, overlaid with thin sheet gold, and a third, inner coffin, in which the mummy lay, which was of pure gold inlaid with semi-precious stones and coloured glazes.

The walls of the burial chamber retain the vividity of colour as on the day they were painted. On the right-hand wall the mummy of the deceased is shown being brought to the tomb by noblemen, one of whom is General Haremhab who later became pharaoh. On the rear wall, Tutankhamon is depicted with the figures of the goddesses of heaven and with Osiris. There is also a unique representation of the 'Opening of the Mouth' ceremony being performed on the deceased king by Aye, who briefly succeeded him to the throne. This ritual was a most ancient one, performed to give the deceased life and power to eat and breathe. On the left-hand wall (a) are symbolic scenes showing the adoration of apes representing the twelve hours of night.

The sarcophagus remains in the burial chamber with the outer of the two wooden coffins containing the decayed mummy of Tutankhamon.

Tomb of Haremhab (57)
This is the tomb of the first pharaoh of non-royal lineage to construct his resting place in the Valley of the Kings. Haremhab was the general who seized control at the end of the 18th Dynasty and his tomb is one of the most remarkable, although the entrance is unimpressive. It slopes through two corridors (1) and (2) that were not completed, but which enable us to see the different stages of mural decoration.

The well-room (3), however, has fine quality reliefs, and the following chamber (4) was actually completed and decorated to resemble a tomb chamber; the stairway to the left rear (a) was carefully concealed, and the plastered wall was painted like the rest of the walls. The robbers were not fooled. The tomb was plundered in antiquity.

The rear corridor (5) is decorated with a series of marvellous paintings showing the deceased Haremhab with Anubis, the jackal-headed god of embalmment and before the various deities, including Hathor, Osiris, Anubis, and Horus son of Isis. In chamber (6), on the left-hand wall (b) he is embraced by Hathor, and stands before Anubis, Isis, Harsiesis (a form of Horus) and Ptah, in turn. On the right-hand wall (c), he is led by Harsiesis to Hathor, and stands before Anubis, Isis, Harsiesis, Hathor, Osiris and Nefertum, in turn. These paintings are of extremely high quality, and in a marvellous state of preservation.

The tomb chamber (7) was never completed. On the higher reaches of the wall there are symbols for north, south, east and west, which were the instructions for workmen who were given appropriate decorations for the different parts of the chamber. These were the hours of the night according to the 'Book of the Gates'.

On the left-hand side of the hall, from (d) to (e) there are scenes from the first hour of the night. Further along, at (f), is the third hour of the night. The missing second hour is depicted on the opposite wall, at (g) and (h).

Towards the rear of the tomb chamber, to the left, is the fourth hour of the night, at (i) and the fifth hour opposite, at (j), where the judgement hall of Osiris is depicted. This is the only full judgement scene in a royal tomb, and it shows Osiris as Lord of the Underworld, with his forty-two judges of the dead, before whom the deceased will answer charges. Having pleaded innocence of all wrong-doing he gains access to a life ever-lasting.

The red granite sarcophagus is beautifully carved with figures of the deities and with religious formulae. At the corners the protective goddesses, Isis and Nephthys, spread their wings to guard the body of the deceased. In the side chamber (8), Osiris is depicted in front of the *Djed* pillar representing rebirth.

Tomb of Ramses VI (9)

This tomb was started by Ramses V and was usurped by his successor. It has three entrance corridors, two chambers, a further two corridors, one after the other in a straight line, leading to the ante-chamber and the tomb chamber. The wall representations are carried out in painted low relief. The standard of craftsmanship is not high, but the tomb chamber has one of the most important ceilings in the Valley of the Kings. In fact, names and mottoes in Coptic and Greek show that this 'Golden Hall' was an attraction from the first century AD.

TOMB OF RAMSES VI (9) Plan 19

TOMB OF HAREMHAB (57)
Plan 18

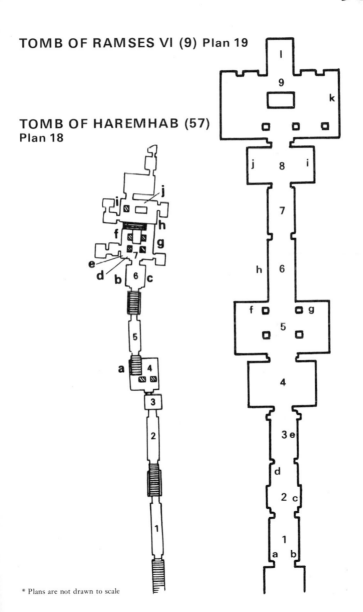

* Plans are not drawn to scale

On each side of the first corridor (1) are representations of the deceased standing before Ra-Harakhte (a) and Osiris (b). On the right-hand wall of the second corridor (c) the barge of the Sun-god travels through the different hours of the night, watched over by Osiris, at (d). The third corridor (3) has the figure of the Sky-goddess Nut extending across the roof, through the ante-chamber (4) and ends in chamber (5). A scene, at (e) shows Osiris under a canopy.

Chamber (5) is supported by four pillars, on each of which the pharaoh is shown making offerings to the deities. On the rear walls (f) and (g) are fine representations of the enthroned Osiris; the deceased burns incense before him. The sloping passage to the rear is guarded by sacred winged snakes.

Deeper and deeper through the different caverns of the under-world we travel, as we pass through corridor (6), which has a fine representation, at (h), of the fourth hour of the night. Protective and sacred emblems safeguard the barge of the Sun-god in the sloping corridor (7), which leads to the ante-chamber. On the right-hand wall (i), the deceased stands with Maat, goddess of Truth; on the left-hand wall (j) are sacred texts.

The tomb chamber (9), which is decorated throughout and is well preserved, has a vaulted ceiling and the smashed sarcophagus at its centre. The right-hand wall (k) has a symbolic representation of the Sun-god represented in the form of a beetle with a ram's head. The boat in which he travels is worshipped by two *bas*, human-headed birds, and by the souls of Kheper and Atum. Above this scene is the goddess Nut, with upstretched arms; below are the condemned, beheaded.

Dark blue and gold predominate on the ceiling, where the goddess Nut is twice depicted along its entire length, in a graceful semi-circle with backs touching. She represents the morning and the evening skies. Her elongated body curves to touch the earth with finger and toe, head to the west and loins to the east. The astrological representations include the different signs of the Egyptian zodiac: lion, serpent, balances, scorpion, archer and goat; the crab, twins, bull, ram, fishes and water carrier. There are also ships containing controllers of the different sections of the day and divisions of the half year.

In the niche to the rear (l), the barge of the Sun-god is held aloft by upstretched arms.

Tomb of Ramses VI

Tomb of Ramses IX (6)

This is a traditional tomb comprising three chambers, one following the other in a straight line. It is approached via an inclined plane with steps on either side. Flanking the doorway are representations of the deceased: he burns incense and makes an offering of a vase to Harmachis-Amon-Ra and to a goddess at (a), and to Amon and Osiris at (b). (The side chambers are undecorated).

On the right-hand wall (c), especially over the second chamber to the right, are some of the weird creatures of the underworld, each represented nine times. This was the sacred number identified with the Nine gods of the Ennead; it also represented the triple-triads. There are nine serpents, nine demons with bull's heads, nine figures surrounded by oval frames and nine human figures with the heads of jackals.

The sacred texts of the sun's journey through the underworld begin here. On the left-hand side of the corridor (d), a priest, in the role of 'Horus who supports his mother', pours the symbols for Life, Health and Prosperity over the deceased pharaoh who is represented in the form of Osiris. The scene symbolically portrays burial rites for the deceased pharaoh in the manner of those performed by Horus and Isis for Osiris in the popular myth.

The second corridor (2) is guarded to left and right (e) by great serpents, rearing themselves to prevent entry through one of the 'Gates of Osiris'. On the left-hand wall (f) is the beginning of another text from the Book of the Dead. The deceased pharaoh is shown advancing into the tomb. In front of him is a goddess who

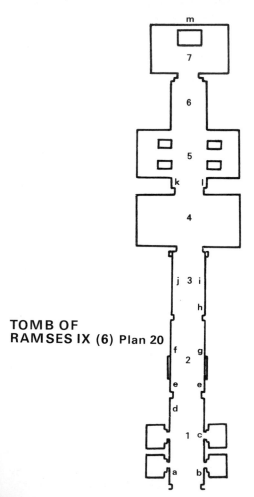

**TOMB OF
RAMSES IX (6) Plan 20**

holds his names to identify him and announce his entrance. He greets (further along the wall) a hawk-headed deity who declares that he will give the deceased pharaoh his 'power, years and seat' in other words, power to be reborn and rule in the afterlife. On the opposite wall (g) are demons and spirits.

Two great guardian serpents guard the entrance to the third corridor (3). On the right-hand wall (h) the pharaoh presents an image of Maat to Ptah of Memphis; beside Ptah stands the goddess Maat herself. Further along is a representation of the mummy of the deceased pharaoh stretched across a mountain. This is a fine symbolic representation of rebirth. Just as the scarab and the sun-disc (represented above) are reborn each morning, so too, would the pharaoh be reborn.

Towards the middle of this same wall at (i) are ritualistic representations, including four men spitting out scarabi as they bend over backwards, demons standing upon serpents, serpents pierced by arrows and the scarab in a boat with two Horus eyes, the most protective of the charms.

On the left-hand wall (j) are the boats of the Sun-god (centre) that travel through the second and third hours of night bearing protective deities.

The passage now opens into a chamber (4). On each side of the doorway leading to the tomb chamber (k) and (l) is a figure clad in a leopard skin. The one on the right is represented with arms raised above the symbolic standard of the ibis, symbol of Thoth the god of Wisdom. That to the left holds a bowl of libation water over the standard of the ram, symbol of Khnum of Elephantine. These figures symbolise the bestowing of Wisdom and Purity on the deceased pharaoh as he approaches the Court of Osiris.

Chamber No. 5 is rough and unfinished. It slopes downwards to the burial chamber through a corridor (6). In the burial chamber (7) there are traces of the sarcophagus on the floor, and on the walls are gods and demons. The goddess Nut, representing the morning and evening skies, is shown across the rough ceiling in two figures. Below are constellations and boats of stars. On the rear wall (m) is the child Horus, seated within the winged sun-disc. This simple symbol represents rebirth after death.

VALLEY OF THE QUEENS

This valley was where some of the queens and royal children of the 19th and 20th Dynasties were buried. There are over twenty tombs;

many are unfinished and entirely without decoration. The most beautiful, that of Nefertari, beloved wife of Ramses II, is not open to visitors. However, we are fortunate that there is another tomb in the same style and with similar representations.

Tomb No. 40

This is the burial place of an unidentified queen. Her tomb so closely resembles that of Nefertari that it is believed to date to the beginning of the 19th Dynasty.

A stairway leads to a large hall, which has two pillars, from which two chambers lead off; one to the rear (south), and one to the right (east). All are beautifully decorated in elaborate low relief, partly filled with stucco and painted in brilliant colours.

To the left of the entrance to the main chamber the deceased queen is seen before a kiosk containing the Anubis jackal, being adored by Nephthys and Isis. This is followed by a beautiful scene of the queen, with an offering, adoring the Hathor cow who emerges from the mountain.

Because of the funerary nature of the wall reliefs of the room to the right, showing scenes of the funeral and the sarcophagus of the deceased, it is thought that this, and not the room to the rear, was the actual burial chamber.

Tomb of Amon-Hir-Khopshef (55)

This son of Ramses III died too young to pass into the divine presence of the gods of the underworld unaccompanied. The scenes show Ramses III leading the nine-year-old youth and introducing him to the various deities. The boy wears a side-lock of hair, indicating youth, and carries the feather of Truth, as he obediently follows his father.

On the left-hand wall of the tomb chamber, travelling clockwise, we see Ramses III, followed by the young prince, offering incense to Ptah (a) and then introducing his son to him. Ramses then presents the boy to Duamutef and to Imseti (b), who conducts the pair to Isis. Note that Isis (c) looks over her shoulder to the advancing pharaoh. She holds him by the hand.

On the right-hand wall Ramses and his son are conducted to Hathor (d), Hapi, Qebsennuef (e), Shu (f) and Nephthys (g), who puts her hand beneath the chin of the bereaved Ramses.

There was no mummy of the boy in the sarcophagus but instead the foetus of a six-month-old child. It is suggested that the Queen was so upset by the death of her son, that she miscarried this baby.

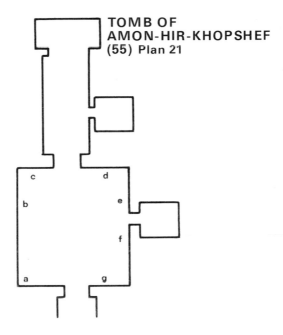

TOMB OF
AMON-HIR-KHOPSHEF
(55) Plan 21

TOMBS OF THE NOBLES

Hundreds of tombs of the nobles were constructed in the foothills of the mountains at the edge of the western desert. The most famous are those at Sheikh Abd el Kurna, west of the Ramesseum. The majority of tombs were designed in two parts: a wide court leading to a hall that was sometimes supported by pillars or columns, and a long corridor to the rear leading to the offering shrine that had niches for the statue of the deceased. The walls were covered with a layer of whitewashed clay; this was painted. There are sculptured reliefs in only a few of the tombs. They shed a flood of light on life in the New Kingdom.

Sheikh Abd el Kurna

Tomb of Nakht (52)

This is a simple tomb of the Scribe of the Granaries under Thutmose IV, who may also have been an astronomer. It comprises two chambers and only the first is decorated. But in this single room are such detailed activities, executed with such infinite charm, and in such good state of repair, that the tomb will always rank as one of the finest.

To the left of the doorway, on the first wall (a), are a series of agricultural scenes including ploughing, digging and sowing. In the upper row the deceased superintends three stages of the harvest: the measuring and winnowing of the grain, the reaping and pressing of the grain into baskets – with a charming drawing of a man leaping in the air so that the weight of his body might press the grain in tightly – and, in the lower row, the labourers being organised by the deceased for ploughing in two teams. Note that the ploughman has ragged hair, the ox is a piebald and that, in the midst of the strenuous work, one of the workers takes a moment's respite to drink from a wineskin on a tree.

On the rear left-hand wall (b) there is a scene showing the deceased and his wife (in the lower row) being brought flowers and geese by their son while three young girls play music to them. These female musicians are sensitively painted in perfect detail. The graceful lute player dances to the accompaniment of a no less graceful flautist and a harpist. The body of one girl is given front-view treatment while her head is turned to speak to her colleague. Above is a blind harpist playing to guests; he is attended by an audience of women seated on the ground – who appear to be gossiping. A young girl leans forward to present perfume before the nostrils of three women.

On the right-hand rear wall (c) the deceased is seated with his wife in an arbour (lower row) while flowers, poultry, grapes and fish are brought to them by their servants.

On this same wall (c) birds are being caught in nets and subsequently plucked. The filled net is a complex of wings and colours. Grapes are being picked and pressed into wine (lower rows), and in the upper row the deceased enjoys his hobbies. He is spearing fish and shooting fowl. The fishing scene was never completed; though the fish themselves are drawn. Nakht has no spear in his hand. His wife tenderly holds an injured bird in her hand. His little daughter holds his leg.

TOMB OF NAKHT (52) Plan 22

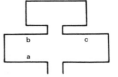

The Tomb of Rekhmire (100)

He was the vizier under Thutmose III and his son, Amenhotep II. It is a traditional 18th Dynasty nobleman's tomb, comprising a narrow, oblong first chamber and a long corridor opposite the entrace. This corridor rapidly gains in height to the rear of the tomb and runs into the rock.

Rekhmire was entrusted with a great many duties. There was nothing, he wrote of himself in an inscription, of which he was ignorant in heaven, on earth or in any part of the underworld. One of the most important scenes in the tomb is to be found on the left-hand wall of the first chamber, near the corner (a). It shows the interior of a court of law in which tax evaders were brought to justice by the vizier himself. The prisoners were led up the central aisle while witnesses waited outside; at the foot of the judgement seat are four mats with rolled papyri. Messengers bow deeply as they enter the presence of Rekhmire.

Near the centre of the opposite wall (b), Rekhmire performs his dual role of receiving taxes from officials who annually came with their dues and tribute from the vassal princes of Asia and the chiefs of Nubia. The foreign gift-bearers are arranged in five rows: from Punt, Crete, Nubia, Syria, and men, women and children from Kush. The tribute ranges from wild animals and animal skins to chariots, pearls and costly vessels.

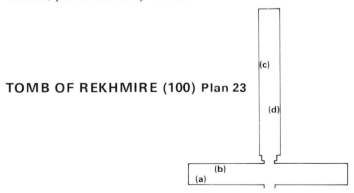

TOMB OF REKHMIRE (100) Plan 23

On the left-hand wall of the inner corridor, at (c), Rekhmire supervises the delivery of grain, wine and cloth from the royal storehouses. He inspects carpenters, leather-workers, metal-workers and potters, who all come under his control. In the lower row is a record of the construction of an entrance portal to the temple of Amon at Karnak showing that Rekhmire supervised the manufacture of the bricks and each stage of the construction.

On the right-hand wall (d) Rekhmire may be seen at a table, and there are scenes of offerings before statues of the deceased, the deceased in a boat on a pond being towed by men on the bank, and a banquet with musicians and singers.

All the representations in this tomb show rhythm. Workers bend to mix mortar or squat to carve a statue. A man raises a bucket to his colleague's shoulder. Another is engrossed in carpentry. The elegant ladies of Rekhmire's household prepare for a social function with young female attendants arranging their hair, anointing their limbs or bringing them jewellery.

The Tomb of Sennofer (96)

In this delightful tomb the entire roof has been painted with a creeping vine. Interesting use has been made of the rough surfaces of the rock to make the grapes and vine-tendrils appear realistic. Both the first small chamber and the main hall, which is supported by four pillars, have been decorated in this manner.

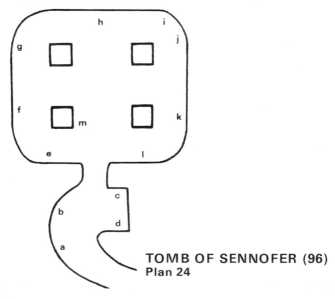

TOMB OF SENNOFER (96)
Plan 24

Sennofer was the Overseer of the Gardens of Amon under Amenhotep II. In his tomb the paintings are in near-perfect condition. A steep flight of stairs takes us down to the first chamber and the first representations we meet, on the left-hand wall (a), show Sennofer being brought offerings from his daughter and ten priests. Circling the chamber clockwise, we see on the two rear walls (b) and (c) drawings of the deceased with his wife worshipping Osiris, who is represented above the doorway of the main chamber. On the right-hand wall (d) the deceased is seen entering and leaving his tomb, while servants bring sacred offerings and his daughter stands behind him.

Above the doorway of the main chamber are two representations of Anubis. Moving clockwise, we come first to a scene of the deceased and his wife emerging from the tomb (e) and, further along, seated on a bench. On the left-hand wall at (f) servants bring furniture to the tomb and set up two obelisks in front of the shrine. At (g) are funerary ceremonies, and the nobleman (to the left) looks on. On the rear wall (h) the deceased and his wife are at a table of offerings, while priests offer sacrifices to the dead.

The symbolic pilgrimage to Abydos (page 19) is depicted at (i). It shows statues of the deceased and his wife in a boat, being towed by another boat.

One of the most beautiful representations is that of the deceased and his wife in an arbour (j) praying to Osiris and Anubis. At (k) a priest clad in a leopard skin purifies them with holy water; at (l) Sennofer, who puts a lotus blossom to his nostrils, is shown before a table of offerings; his wife tenderly holds his leg.

The Tomb of Menna (69)

This fine tomb belongs to the Scribe of the Fields under Thutmose IV. It is in a good state of preservation, apart from the face of Menna which has been deliberately destroyed.

On the left-hand entrance wall (a) Menna can be seen before a table of offerings. Further along at (b) are agricultural scenes: grain being measured, recorded, winnowed and trodden. The ploughing and sowing is followed by reaping. A young girl removes a thorn from a friend's foot (bottom row), and two girls quarrel (immediately above). At (c) Menna watches a ship docking with a cargo of stores.

On the left-hand wall of the rear corridor (d) are funerary scenes of the pilgrimage to Abydos in fine detail and brilliant colour. Menna's heart is weighed before Osiris (the tongue of the balance

TOMB OF MENNA (69) Plan 25

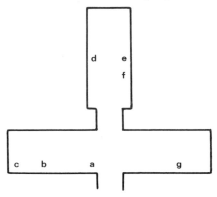

has been destroyed). On the right-hand wall (e) is the famous fishing and fowling scene among the papyrus thickets. The deceased nobleman is enjoying his favourite pastime. Coloured fowl rise from the rushes. Crocodile, duck and assorted fish are in the water. Menna's daughter kneels to pluck a lotus flower from the rushes but his throwing stick has been deliberately cut through.

To the right of the fishing scene (f) is a ship (top row) from which one of the sailors leans over the side to fill a vessel with water from the river. The right-hand entrance wall (g) shows that Menna usurped this tomb, covering the original reliefs with stucco and redecorating it, hence the deliberate damage to his face, presumably done by relatives of the original owner.

The Tomb of Ramose (55)
This tomb belongs to the vizier in the reigns of Amenhotep III and IV (later Akhenaten). It comprises a main hall with thirty-two rather squat papyrus columns (1), an inner hall (2) containing eight clustered columns of smaller dimension (all destroyed), and the shrine (3).

The tomb of Ramose is of historical importance because it is one of the few standing monuments in Luxor of the period of transition from the worship of Amon-Ra to that of the Aten under Akhenaten. The tomb gives us a unique opportunity to see conventional 18th Dynasty representations alongside the realism that is associated with the Amarna period.

The reliefs to left and right of the entrance doorway are in the conventional style, typical of the beginning of Amenhotep IV's reign. To the left (a), Ramose sits with his relatives, all of whom wear elaborate wigs. The figures are unpainted apart from the eyes. To the right (b) are scenes of worship, offerings and religious ceremonies.

Another traditional representation is on the left-hand rear wall (c), which shows Amenhotep IV in stylised, customary treatment; he had not yet changed his name to Akhenaten or moved the capital to Tel el Amarna. He sits beneath a canopy with Maat, goddess of Truth. Ramose himself is twice represented before the throne.

On the right-hand rear wall (d) we see the young pharaoh, who stands with his royal consort Nefertiti on a balcony, depicted in the Amarna style and attitude (page 118). Ramose is being decorated with gold chains. Akhenaten is portrayed with his belly extended, in unflattering realism. Above the figures is the life-giving sun, the Aten, with fourteen rays; four of them hold symbols of Life and Happiness. Two support Akhenaten's outstretched arm. Another offers the symbol of Life to the nostrils of the queen.

On the left-hand wall (e) is an expressive relief of a group of mourners. Grief comes down the centuries in a heart-rending funerary convoy. The men carry boxes covered with foliage, a jar of water and flowers. A group of grieving women turn towards the funeral bier and fling their arms about; tears stream down their cheeks. One woman is supported by a sympathetic attendant; others beat their breasts and thighs in grief or squat to gather dust to scatter on their heads as a sign of bereavement.

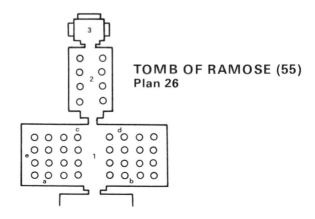

TOMB OF RAMOSE (55)
Plan 26

TOMB OF USERHET (56) Plan 27

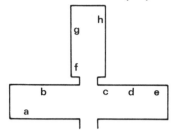

Tomb of Userhet (56)

This tomb, situated near that of Ramose, belongs to a royal scribe in the reign of Amenhotep II, and the paintings are extremely well preserved. On the left-hand entrance wall there are rural scenes. These include the inspection and branding of cattle, overthrowing bulls, and the collection of grain. The rear left-hand wall (b) is partly destroyed. It shows the deceased feasting with members of his family. He is offered a necklace and a cup, and his son brings a bouquet of flowers.

On the right-hand rear wall (c), bags of gold-dust are being counted in the upper registers, and, below, is a delightful scene of the inspection of recruits; men, including barbers, are seated beneath the tree. Further along the wall bakers make bread (d) and the deceased Userhet, in a colourful red tunic with yellow spots, makes offerings to his pharaoh (e).

In the inner corridor, there is a spirited hunting scene at (f), in which the nobleman, in his chariot, shoots at fleeing animals in the desert; these include gazelles, hares and hyena. Userhet has the reins tied around his waist and the string of his bow taut and ready to shoot. At (g) is a scene of weeping women. The rest of the right-hand wall is taken up with a funeral procession including a chariot, horse and river vessels. (In the niche to the rear of the corridor are statues of the owner and his wife.)

Deir el Medina:

Tomb of Sennudjem (1)

This is the tomb of the Servant in the Place of Truth in the reign of Ramses II. A narrow flight of stairs leads us to a single chamber with a low curved roof. Opposite the entrance are two particularly noteworthy scenes. To the left Anubis, god of embalming, leans over the mummy of the deceased which lies on a lion-headed couch, and Osiris is depicted before an offering table flanked by two protective Horus eyes. To the right, is a fine, formal funerary feast with the presentation of offerings and perfumes, and the deceased being led by Anubis.

The roof is decorated with scenes showing the opening of the door of the tomb, the journey through the underworld and different chapters from the mortuary literature. The delightful agricultural scene on the right-hand wall, showing ripe wheat fields, fruits and flowers, is undoubtedly a vision of what Sennudjem hoped to enjoy in the afterlife.

Tomb of Pashedu (3)

Pashedu was the Servant in the Place of Truth under the later Ramessides. A steep staircase leads to a vaulted corridor, with Anubis depicted on each wall, and the burial chamber where the sarcophagus, unusually made of limestone slabs rather than a single block of stone, stood against the rear wall.

The two long walls are decorated with conventional scenes of Pashedu and his relatives adoring the gods. The most noteworthy scene is on the right hand entrance wall, where the deceased crouches in prayer beside a decorative palm-tree which grows by the side of the lake.

Tomb of Inherkhau (359)

This tomb belongs to the artistic supervisor of the necropolis in the 20th Dynasty. Its decoration, not surprisingly, is extremely good, especially in the innermost chamber where the deceased is depicted with a group of his grandchildren receiving a statuette of Osiris and a box containing a *shawabti* figure. He is also depicted with his wife holding candles and listening to a harp-player.

On the right-hand wall Inherkhau can be seen adoring two lions, guardians of the two horizons which came to represent Today and Tomorrow.

Asasif:

Tomb of Kheru-ef (192)

This is the tomb of the steward to the Great Royal Wife Queen Tiy, wife of Amenhotep III. It was never completed, but it is interesting to observe that, while other noblemen of the 18th Dynasty, like

110

TOMB OF KHERU-EF
Plan 28

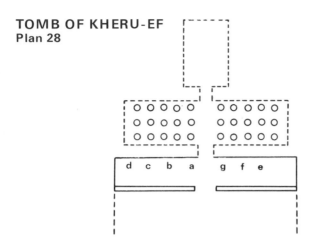

Ramose for example, abandoned Thebes and went to the new capital of Tel el Amarna, Kheru-ef remained on, and served the royal mother. Also interesting is that a hymn to Amon-Ra laid out in crossword fashion (which is effaced but has been carefully re-established by scholars) shows Amenhotep IV (later Akhenaten) adoring Ra-Harakhte, and offering libations to Amenhotep III, his father, and Queen Tiy.

The reliefs are finely carved. On the left-hand wall, on the outer lintel, the royal couple adore the deities, and the texts on the jambs mention the parents of the deceased. At (a) is a processional dance in their honour. At (b) and (c) the deceased is being rewarded; he stands with officials before the pharaoh the goddess Hathor and Queen Tiy in a kiosk. Towards the end of the wall (d) are delightful representations of the *Heb-Sed* jubilee. The royal couple are depicted in a boat, and also shown leaving the palace. Eight slim princesses bearing vases with sacred water, walk in pairs. There are female dancers, jugglers and priests.

On the right-hand wall, at (e) the royal couple raise the *Djed* pillar of Osiris amidst great celebration. There are male and female dancers, singers and offering-bearers. Boats bring provisions and butchers, cattle and donkeys are driven round the walls of Memphis; the latter was a most ancient tradition. At (f) and (g) the deceased is represented in another *Heb-Sed* festival, in which he offers a decorative floral vase and necklaces to the royal couple, and Nine Bows, representing the conquered territories.

III

Other monuments in Luxor:

I 12

TEL EL AMARNA AKET-ATEN 'THE HORIZON OF ATEN' Plan 29

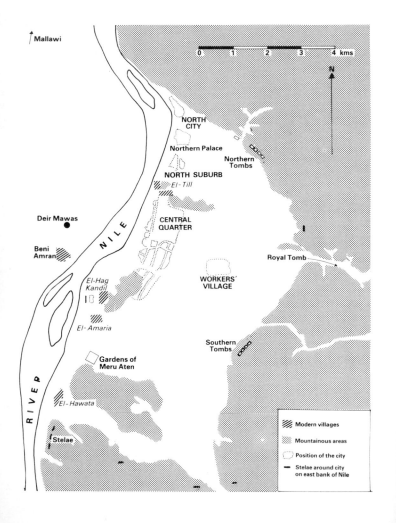

CHAPTER 4   TEL EL AMARNA (AKHET-ATEN 'THE HORIZON OF ATEN')

The north tombs of Akhet-Aten

BACKGROUND

On the eastern bank of the Nile, across the river from the modern village of Deir Mawas, is a large crescent-shaped plain over four kilometres long and about 800 metres broad. This was the site of *Akhet-Aten*, 'The Horizon of Aten', chosen by the pharaoh Akhenaten (*c.* 1375–1350 BC) for his new capital. It was a site that had no history of cult activity. That is to say, there was no earlier settlement or existing priesthood.

Unlike other cities in ancient Egypt, *Akhet-Aten* was built not in the fertile valley but on a barren plain. The agricultural land lay on the western bank of the Nile. The city had no enclosure wall. Yet it is evident from tomb reliefs that there were strong detachments of troops who guarded the royal family and undoubtedly patrolled the desert slopes.

The three main streets of the city ran parallel to the river. The central quarter, which spread southwards from the modern village of el-Till to that of el-Hag Kandil, was the main residential area and also the site of the temple of the Aten. To the north and south were habitations for officials and priests. The side streets contained smaller houses for the middle class and for servants. The working class, especially those employed on the necropolis, lived in special compounds to the east of the plain. They were built on parallel streets and were uniform and comfortable, with one larger house to each compound. This probably belonged to the supervisor.

Worship of the Aten

In the worship of the sun disc, the Aten, some scholars have seen metaphysical reasoning far ahead of the times. Others have asserted that it offered nothing new. Akhenaten himself has been variously interpreted as a mystic/ascetic and as a rebel/fanatic. Certainly, to understand Akhenaten and the brief epoch of sun worship, we must place it in the broad context of the 18th Dynasty. This was a time when the Egyptian empire extended to its greatest extent and when, to all outward appearances, it was at its most stable.

In fact, there were undercurrents of discontent. A new warrior society had emerged from the humiliation of the Hyksos occupation. Great conquerors like Thutmose III had extended Egypt's borders to embrace a vast empire. As a result, tribute and booty poured into Thebes. Naturally most of the wealth was bestowed upon Amon-Ra, the god of the victors, and the priests consequently came to control undreamed of material rewards. They and the cult that they promoted became tarnished by self-interest. Amenhotep IV, as he was first known, grew up in an atmosphere geared to change. His father was Amenhotep III (with whom he may have shared a co-regency) and his mother was the Great Royal Wife, Queen Tiy.

The concept of the Aten (*Itn*), which means 'the sun's disc', was not invented by Akhenaten. His grandfather, Thutmose IV recorded on a commemorative scarab (in the British Museum) that he fought a campaign in Asia '. . . with the Aten before (him) . . . to make the foreigners to be like true people (i.e. Egyptians) in order to serve the Aten forever'.* And in the reign of his father, Amenhotep III, the term *Aten* first came into prominent use at Thebes.

Worship of the sun, in one form or another, is apparent throughout ancient Egyptian history. The pharaoh himself was regarded as 'son of the Sun-god'; important local deities, like Amon, Min and Khnum, under the influence of the solar worship, bore the

*J. Wilson, *Burden of Egypt*, OUP 1961 p.210.

sun disc on their heads and appended 'Ra' to their names. Daily temple rituals were oriented to the sun. The representation of Ra-Harakhtc, 'Horus of the Horizon', which was the traditional form of the Sun-god, was a hawk crowned with the sun disc; it is, therefore, significant that the Aten, like the national god Amon-Ra, was represented as such. It was only later that the hawk gave way to the solar disc with slanting rays ending in hands.

Akhenaten and the Aten with slanting rays (Cairo Museum)

It would appear that the priests of Amon at Thebes at first saw no danger in allowing worship of the solar disc. They permitted several sun temples to be constructed within the sacred precincts of Amon's temple complex at Karnak. The main difference that can be discerned between worship of Amon-Ra and the Aten in the early stages, was a vibrant call to draw the attention of worshippers away from the darkened sanctuaries of Amon-Ra toward the light of day. Stress was placed on *Maat* (Truth/Order) in a desire to free religious rites from the shackles of superstition encouraged by the priests of Amon and to revert to a more purified form of sun worship. In other words the people were encouraged to turn from the darkened sanctuaries of 'The Hidden One' (i.e. Amon) and worship the visible, unapproachable orb directly beneath the open sky.

In the sixth year of Amenhotep IV's reign, the status quo drastically changed. He announced the founding of his new city, changed his name to Akhenaten ('Splendour of the Aten') and promulgated a decree that henceforth one god, the Aten, should be worshipped. He officially ordered the closing of all the temples of Amon. He gave instructions that the possessions of the state priesthood should be confiscated and that all statues of the national deity should be destroyed.

The massive temples of honour of Amon-Ra could not be dismantled but Akhenaten ordered the name of 'Amon' be effaced from the reliefs. His workers applied themselves to the task with exaggerated zeal, scoring out Amon's name at the top of Hatshepsut's lofty obelisk at Karnak and even the royal 'cartouche' of Akhenaten's father, Amenhotep III.

Two years later, in the eighth year of his reign, Akhenaten, his Queen Nefertiti (whose name was extended to include the new epithet – Nefernefern*aten*), and their two daughters (later there were six) took up residence at *Akhet-Aten*. Akhenaten set up boundary stelae on the cliffs on both sides of the Nile; they recorded an oath in the name of his 'father' the Aten that neither he, his wife, nor his children would pass the limits he was setting and that the land would be sacred to the Aten forever.

Worship of the Aten was not so much a new realm of thought as a revision of traditional beliefs toward recognition of the unlimited power of the Sun-god. The religion of the Aten should not be regarded as a sudden outburst of spiritual inspiration. In a forever expanding world, religious concepts change. In Akhenaten's reign sun worship was lifted from the suffocating cloak of accumulated ritual, spells, oracles and all the awesome journeys through monster-infested subterranean channels of the underworld. It was worship of the sun disc in the open, calling on the Aten as the creator and preserver of mankind.

Akhenaten's celebrated hymn

The much celebrated hymn that is inscribed in the Tomb of Aye (page 123) has been ascribed to Akhenaten himself:

'. . . .O living Aten, beginner of life when thou didst shine forth in the eastern horizon, and didst fill every land with thy beauty. . . . Being afar off, yet thy rays are upon the earth. Thou art in men's faces, yet thy movements are unseen . . . . The earth grows bright, when thou hast arisen in the horizon . . . . The Two Lands are in festival . . . . The entire land does its work. All cattle are at peace upon their pastures. Trees and pastures grow green. Birds taking flight from their nest, their wings give praise to thy spirit. All animals frisk upon their feet . . . . the fish in the river leap before thy face. Who causest the male fluid to flow in women and who maketh the water in mankind; bringing to life the son in the body of the mother; soothing him by the cessation of his tears . . . . The chick in the egg speaketh in the shell; thou givest him air in it to make him live . . . . How manifold are thy works. They are mysterious in men's sight. Thou sole god, like to whom there is no other. Thou didst create the earth after thy heart, being alone, even all men, herds and flocks, whatever is upon earth, creatures that walk upon feet, which soar aloft flying with their wings, the countries of Khor [Palestine and Syria] and of Cush [Sudan], and the land of Egypt . . . .'[1]

In about the fourteenth year of Akhenaten's reign, Nefertiti took up residence in her northern palace, and shortly afterwards Akhenaten appointed Smenkhare, his half-brother, as co-regent[2] Akhenaten died, as did Smenkhare almost immediately, and Tutankhaten (later Tutankhamon) came to the throne. This boy-king, probably another half-brother of Akhenaten, restored the worship of Amon and transferred the capital back to Thebes.

The city of *Akhet-Aten*, still under construction, was totally razed. All that was left were a few walls and columns of no more than a metre high. It is from these ruins and from the ground-plans that

[1] (Extracts from the translation by Sir A. Gardiner, *Egypt of the Pharaohs*, Clarendon Press, Oxford, p. 225/226.)
[2] In a lecture given in March 1982, James Allen, then Director of the American Research Center in Egypt, presented evidence to support the theory that Nefertiti, not Smenkare, may have shared a co-regency with Akhenaten for some years and consequently succeeded him as pharaoh (i.e. that it is Nefertiti dressed as a pharaoh, or Smenkhare, who is depicted on reliefs).

archaeologists have been able to study city-planning in ancient Egypt. Elsewhere the palaces, temples and dwelling-places, which were built of sun-dried brick in the Nile valley, perished. The city at Tel el Amarna, however, which was constructed on a plain above the flood and occupied for little more than a decade, provides one of the best opportunities to study how the people in an ancient Egyptian city actually lived.

Little wonder that Tel el Amarna can claim to be one of the most thoroughly explored sites in Egypt. Work was started there in 1911 and continues to the present day.

The Art of the 'Amarna Period'

For thousands of years the pharaoh had ruled as a god and was portrayed as great, powerful and majestic. Whether sculpted massively for temple entrance, or shown being crowned, honoured and adored in temple relief, he was symbolically depicted as a giant. He clasped captives by their long hair as a hunter holds his game; he raised his club above his prisoners as a champion above his fallen opponent. The cult of divine kingship was based on the understanding that the God-king was more than a man.

During the so-called Amarna Period, Akhenaten was depicted quite naturalistically. The movement apparent in the surviving reliefs contrasts with the chiselled outlines of earlier works. Naturalism broke with the overpowering formality of the past. The pharaoh was often shown the same size as his people. He was a mortal; flesh of human flesh, bone of human bone. He was not aloof and alone but one who moved in their very midst. He was an ordinary man, a family man, who could delight in his daughters, eat a hearty meal, and demonstrate tender affection.

Akhenaten's chief sculptor Bak, who set the style of the Amarna art, claimed to have been an apprentice to the king himself. It seems that Akhenaten wished to exaggerate his physical imperfections in order to emphasise a pharaoh who was a mortal; just as representations of earlier pharaohs portrayed the physically perfect god.

Akhenaten's brooding eyes were exaggerated into heavy-lidded slits. His shapely, sensitive lips were magnified. His lean face, receding forehead and thin neck became an elongated skull, drawn-in cheeks and an arching neck. Akhenaten's soft belly was made pendulous, his thighs and buttocks overly thick, and his arms and legs spindly. Humanizing the pharaoh, with all his imperfections, appears to have been the main issue in the Amarna art.

There are two dozen enormous so-called 'sexless' statues of

Akhenaten that were unearthed from Karnak and are dated to the early years of his rule. They are of obscure, symbolic meaning. On some, not all, Akhenaten is shown wearing no robe or kilt, yet, apart from the heavy breasts, there is an absence of sex organs. No pharaoh had ever before been sculpted this way. The only deity similarly represented was Hapi, the Nile-god, whose bulbous breasts symbolised fertility, but who always wore a kilt.

One plausable explanation may be that the tradition of kingship was so closely associated with the fertility of the land that Akhenaten could not ignore it. However, instead of being associated with such fertility gods as the ithyphallic god Min or the ram god Khnum, he chose to be portrayed similar to Hapi, the one god associated with water and fertility who was not a member of a triad.

Be that as it may, the state artists worked on themes approved by the pharaoh and were free at last to portray him as realistically as they themselves had been portrayed in tomb reliefs – in a wide variety of activities and shown in free, relaxed poses. Here was a leader with a great love of nature, who could weep at the death of his daughter and be shown in tender, personal relationships with his family. He rode around the state capital in an open chariot, with streamers flying, and happily waving his hand. He was the teacher of the new faith. In many a nobleman's tomb we see statements such as '. . . how prosperous is he who listens to thy teaching . . .' or '. . . great is a servant who hears thy teaching . . .'

Fragments of slabs carved in relief were found in many homes at Tel el Amarna. They show the figures of Akhenaten, Nefertiti and their children making offerings to the Aten. They were the blessed family who served as an example, and the message is clear: adore the one whom Akhenaten adores and make offerings directly to the one to whom Akhenaten makes offerings. In a stele, which had been reused in Cairo, Akhenaten and Nefertiti, together with their sick daughter Meket-Aten, are shown prostrating themselves on the ground before the Aten in a unique gesture of humility (or perhaps pleading for her recovery). The people were shown, by simple example, to appeal directly to the source and the preserver of life – the sun, the Aten.

DESCRIPTION

The Aten Temple Complex

The gigantic Temple of Aten was situated in the central quarter of the city. The main sanctuary was more than 1500 metres in length. It was surrounded by a wall enclosing a huge open courtyard, and the entrance faced towards the east. Within the complex were other buildings, including the 'Gem of Aten' and the 'House of Rejoicing'. The main temple was called *Het Ben-ben* or Temple of the *Ben-ben*, which referred to the pyramidon, the sacred symbol of the sun cult from earlier times at Heliopolis.

Fashionable villas

The inhabitants of Tel el Amarna were mostly refined citizens who lived in large, carefully planned houses. They were usually surrounded by a wall. Inscriptions on the door-frames contained the names of the owners. The front part, which was approached by a door in the side wall, led to a large traverse hall, which often led up to a north-oriented balcony with wooden pillars. Here petitioners would gather, and there was accommodation for servants.

In the main building was a large reception hall; its roof was supported by wooden columns. It was spacious and airy, with light filtering through windows placed high up near the ceiling. To the rear of the hall was a niche, approached by a raised step, provided with a stone basin for ablutions. (In similar niches in the houses of some officials was a sort of family altar that held a small stela of the royal family.)

Behind the reception hall were sleeping quarters. The bedrooms had raised alcoves for the beds. Bathrooms had basins, water containers and toilets; they adjoined the bedrooms. Even the most humble houses at Tel el Amarna were equipped with similar hygienic facilities.

To the rear of the sleeping quarters were the chambers for the women, with separate bathrooms. In the most palatial houses, there was often a separate upstairs balcony where members of the household could enjoy the north breeze and sleep in the outdoors, if so desired.

Each house had the cooking quarters, offices and storerooms set apart from the living quarters. Gardening appears to have been a great pleasure of the upper classes, and the gardens often had ornamental ponds that, in some cases, were decorated with statues or with a kiosk nearby. There were also cattle stalls and poultry houses.

After a few years of occupation, when construction of the central quarter was still under way, summer palaces and country houses were constructed for members of the royal family and for the nobility outside the main city. In the vicinity of the so-called Northern Palace was an aviary and a zoo; its walls were decorated with paintings of bird-life. The summer-house of Meru-Aten, to the south, had halls, decorative pools and floors painted with animals and plant life.

Builders, architects and sculptors were, of course, among the most respected inhabitants at Tel el Amarna. Sculptors particularly so, because there was a great demand for statues and reliefs of the royal family. It was in the house of the chief sculptor Thutmose that the famous bust of Nefertiti in the Berlin Museum was found. It was one of many models of heads; some were still standing on the shelf, others had fallen or appear to have been deliberately broken. Nefertiti's head shows her to have been truly 'Fair of Face', which was one of her epithets.

There are two groups of nobleman's tombs at Tel el Amarna. They are hewn out of separate rock formations on the eastern bank of the Nile, to the north and south of the city, and each is approached from the plain. The tombs are decorated with reliefs, and apart from the foundations of the temples and buildings in the plain, it is from these reliefs that archaeologists have been provided with fuller detail about the elevation and decoration of the buildings of the capital, especially of the royal palace. Though the reliefs were hacked at and spoiled after the return of the capital to Thebes – some had never been completed – they nevertheless fill in many gaps in our knowledge of life at *Akhet-Aten*

Tombs – General
The design of the tombs at Tel el Amarna are similar to the 18th Dynasty tombs at Luxor. Each has a forecourt (originally surrounded by a brick wall), a main chamber hewn out of rock and sometimes supported by columns, and an inner chamber, or chambers, containing a statue of the deceased.

Near the entrance doorway of each tomb and also in the main chamber, there are usually representations of the royal family praying or making offerings to the Aten and receiving the symbols of life from 'the arm of the sun beams'. Nefertiti usually wears a tall crown, not unlike the blue war crown worn by Akhenaten. Noteworthy is the fact that she and the royal children, as well as some of the noblemen, were depicted with thick thighs and thin necks, indicating that such proportions became fashionable.

Northern Tombs

Tomb of Huye (1)
This tomb belongs to the superintendent of the royal harem and

steward of the Queen Mother, Tiÿ, who is depicted in the doorway reciting the Hymn to the Sun. The reliefs are in fair condition. To the right of the **entrance wall** are representations of a banquet where Akhenaten and Nefertiti are seated opposite Amenhotep III and Queen Tiy. Below is a delightful representation of two princesses facing each other. Above the royal couple is the symbol of the Aten. Guards stand to the right. Musicians and servants are depicted below.

The **main chamber** has two clustered papyrus columns. The scene on the *right-hand* wall shows the temple with colonnaded court, statues and altar, with Akhenaten leading his mother to her Sun-shade Temple. The *left-hand* wall depicts Akhenaten being borne in a carrying chair to the temple with a large retinue of officials.

On each side of the doorway in the rear wall, Akhenaten is shown on the balcony of the palace throwing gifts to Huya. Below, to the right, is the workshop of a sculptor who is painting a statuette of the princess Baketaten, Tiy's daughter. The inner chambers were unfinished.

Tomb of Meri-Re (4)

This is one of the largest and most well preserved tombs belonging to the high priest of the Aten, also known as 'Beloved of Ra'. The roof of the **main chamber** was originally supported by four columns. Moving anti-clockwise, we follow scenes (right of the doorway) of Akhenaten at a palace window, casting forth golden ornaments to Meri-Re. On the left-hand wall he is in his chariot, driving from his palace (above) to the Temple of Aten. Leading the chariot are guards. Following him are the queen, the princesses and escorts; some are in chariots and some on foot.

On the *rear wall* priests await the arrival of the royal procession at the temple. (Note the storehouses, barns and other chambers enclosed in a garden.) Having completed their prayers, the royal couple emerges from the palace (*right-hand wall*) to be greeted by priests. In the lower row the royal couple inspect the storehouses.

On *the left-hand* entrance wall is a scene of the royal pair, accompanied by their daughters, worshipping the Aten. Meri-Re and another priest stand beside the altar. Also present are the royal retinue and priests. On the lower reaches of the wall blind singers are borne in two carriages.

Southern Tombs
Tomb of Mahu (9)
This is the tomb of a police officer, which is entered by a narrow flight of steps. In the main chamber Mahu is represented on all four walls carrying out his official duties. As we move anti-clockwise, we see him supervising the delivery of produce and lending an ear to his officials. On the right-hand wall is a scene that starts at the centre and continues on the rear wall; it depicts the king and queen in a chariot being guided on a tour of the police quarters by Mahu himself.

The scene, starting at the centre of the left-hand wall and continuing on the rear wall, shows men kneeling in prayer before the Temple of Aten. The deceased himself is in the lower register. At the top of the wall the royal couple drive from the palace, preceded by runners. Immediately below, we see them on the return journey.

Tomb of Aye (25)
Aye was known as 'Divine Father'. He was the husband of Queen Nefertiti's nurse. Among his many titles was 'Overseer of All the Horses of His Majesty'. He was Akhenaten's close friend and adviser, a role he continued with the young pharaoh Tutankhamon.

When Tel el Amarna was abandoned after Akhenaten's death, Aye's tomb was incomplete. It is clear, however, that it was planned to be one of the most imposing on the necropolis.

The representations on the entrance doorposts, the entrance to the main chamber and on the four completed columns (of the twenty-four originally intended in the main hall) are of Akhenaten, Nefertiti and the royal children, as well as Aye and Ti, his wife, praying to the Aten. It was in this tomb that the most complete version of the Hymn to the Sun (page 117) was found. It was inscribed on the right-hand side of the entrance doorway.

The most noteworthy scene is to be found to the left of the entrance doorway. Though damaged, it is a vivid and detailed scene showing gold chains and decorations being thrown from the window of the palace by Akhenaten and Nefertiti to Aye and his wife Ti. Beside Nefertiti are three princesses, one of whom affectionately touches her mother's chin. In the upper register are sentries. In the palace courtyard are chariots, scribes, fan-bearers, soldiers, visitors and dancers. The officials either bend in respect or raise their hands in homage to the royal family. Aye himself emerges from the palace (to the right), and his retainers and friends congratulate him for the honours paid him.

Akhenaten's Tomb

There is a large tomb complex situated over five kilometres due east of Tel el Amarna, which is approached from the valley between the northern and southern groups of tombs. It was ravished after the death of Akhenaten and is not open to the general public. Recent studies have led Egyptologists to believe that the complex was originally intended for the entire royal family, which would make it unique among royal tombs. Also, it is believed that Akhenaten was buried there, though his body has not been found.

Few reliefs remain. One is a scene expressing great sorrow by Akhenaten, Nefertiti and the whole court, at the death of the princess Meket-Aten.

Akhenaten's boundary stele at Tuna el-Gebel

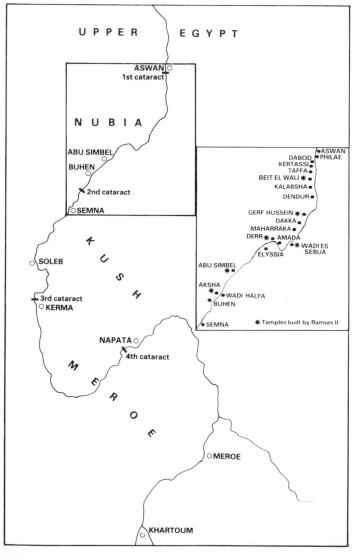

NUBIA AND KUSH Plan 30

UPPER EGYPT

ASWAN
1st cataract

NUBIA

ABU SIMBEL
BUHEN
2nd cataract
SEMNA

K U S H

SOLEB
3rd cataract
KERMA

M E R O E

NAPATA
4th cataract

MEROE

KHARTOUM

ASWAN
PHILAE
DABOD
KERTASSI
TAFFA
BEIT EL WALI
KALABSHA
DENDUR
GERF HUSSEIN
DAKKA
MAHARRAKA
DERR AMADA
WADI ES
SEBUA
ELYSSIA
ABU SIMBEL
AKSHA
WADI HALFA
BUHEN
SEMNA

✳ Temples built by Ramses II

CHAPTER 5   ABU SIMBEL AND THE MONUMENTS OF NUBIA

BACKGROUND

Historical perspective of Nubia and Kush

Egypt and Nubia were culturally linked from earliest times. In fact, there is evidence that Nubia was populated in pre-history by tribes under regional chieftains, much as the earliest settlers in Upper Egypt. The excavation from Nubian tombs of objects of Egyptian origin, such as stone storage vessels, cornelian, amethyst and faience beads, indicate cultural exchange and diffusion from earliest times.

During the Old Kingdom, as we have seen from the rock tombs of Aswan (page 42), there seems to have been a loose sovereignty over Nubia. The people, moving with their herds of sheep and goats, relied on Egypt for grain and vegetable oil. And, well aware of the rich veins of gold-bearing quartz and iron ore in this seemingly impoverished land, Egypt was only too happy to supply their requirements.

Skirmishes with border tribes were not infrequent, and there is evidence of Egypt taking Nubian prisoners and confiscating cattle. But on the whole relations seem to have been friendly, and a state of mutual respect existed. Nubians travelled across the border into Egypt, even as far northwards as Dendera. They usually helped the Egyptians in the transportation of goods when the noblemen of Elephantine were trading with the south. And they were also recruited, on occasion, to help the Egyptian troops suppress rebellious bedouin tribes in Lower Egypt. In a decree written by Pepi I (*c.* 2300 BC) he makes several references to 'the peaceful Nubians'.

Only in the Middle Kingdom (2133–1786 BC) did Nubia lose its independent status. Amenemhet I built a fortress at Semna. Amenemhet II established a trading post as far south as Kerma. And finally Senusert III fixed the southern frontier of Egypt at Semna, just above the Second Cataract. At this point, the Nile thundered through a gap in the granite barrier and provided a natural control point; it also provided a physical environment that closely resembled that just south of Elephantine.

The great fortresses of Semna and Buhen were constructed on natural elevations; they were two of a possible half dozen other fortresses. Through its domination of Nubia, the Egyptians were not only assured of the produce from this great gold and copper-producing country, but were also in an ideal position to trade for other prized commodities further south.

Kush (Sudan), unlike its northern neighbour Nubia, was fertile. It was also rich in natural resources. Its people, the *Mejay*, were vigorous and courageous and strongly resisted the Egyptian occupation of Nubia. It was Senusert III who finally suppressed them. His army was aided by Nubians, who were so delighted that they celebrated the victory by turning Senusert into a national hero. A great temple was built in his honour, and this became the site of a flourishing Egyptian community. After his death Senusert was deified and worshipped for centuries later.

Generation after generation of Egyptian soldiers and settlers lived in or around the fortress towns of Nubia, slowly spreading their traditions and religious beliefs. During the Hyksos occupation of Egypt many of the fortresses were burned or abandoned, but after the war of liberation, the leaders of the New Kingdom (1567–1080 BC) turned their attention once again towards Nubia and Kush.

Thutmose I pushed the frontier south of Semna to 'valleys not known to my ancestors'. The territory flourished, and many fine structures were raised on or around the sites of the earlier fortresses. Among these was a temple at Buhen, built by Hatshepsut (later claimed by her successor Thutmose III, who also restored the temple of his deified ancestor Senusert III). Amenhotep III and his Queen Tiy built a splendid temple at Soleb, on the same plan and in the same style as the Temple of Luxor (page 55). At nearby Sesibi Akhenaten built a temple. Viceroys were appointed to govern there and ensure the regularity of the annual tribute to the treasury.

By the 19th Dynasty Egyptian influence had spread southwards to the Fourth Cataract, and Napata became yet another settlement. Lower Nubia (Egyptian Nubia) was by now a mere geographical extension of Egypt and settlement in Upper Nubia and Kush was strongly encouraged. With the establishment of large communities, not only were Egypt's technological skills introduced far southwards, but its religious tradition as well.

It is noteworthy that Nubian and Kushite nobility were treated with due respect, and some of the tombs at Luxor depict handsome princes standing beautifully attired in a procession to the state capital. A scene in the tomb of Amenhotep-Huy, viceroy of Kush in Tutankhamon's reign, shows the tribute from Kush being presented to Huy by a large number of officials, including a princess of Kush in person. She travelled in her own chariot, protected by a sunshade and accompanied by a retinue.

These were peaceful times when even the nomadic desert tribes, usually a problem, were suppressed. The Medjay, who had long been recognised for their fighting ability, helped law enforcement in the Nile valley and even strengthened pharaoh's armies in Asia.

Ramses II, that most prolific of temple builders, constructed six temples in Nubia between the First and Second Cataracts (Map page 126). Due to the scanty strip of valley, all were hewn out of the rocky outcrops overlooking the river. Some had free-standing statues leading from the cliff face to the river bank. Each must have had a sizeable community to support it. The stress on temples and trade, rather than on fortresses with military garrisons, was a testimonial to the solidarity of Egyptian control of its southern possession, which were by this time totally imbued with the culture of Egypt.

A change only occurred in the status of Lower Nubia in the reign of Ramses XII (1080 BC) when the high priest Hrihor became viceroy of Kush. His control of the south gave him the wealth and military might to usurp the throne of Egypt. He declared himself to be Pharaoh of Upper and Lower Egypt. But, in fact, Lower Egypt was at that time ruled by a strong family in Tanis in the Delta. Divided rule meant weakened rule, and in the confusion following Hrihor's death, Kush became increasingly independent while, in Egypt, there was a steady decline and almost total disregard for law and order.

During these unstable years a family of Libyan descent acquired power. They were probably the descendants of captured prisoners and voluntary settlers granted land in return for military service. They took over leadership and ruled Egypt for two centuries, from 940 to 730 BC.

Meanwhile, deep in the land of Kush, Napata became the focal point of a new kingdom. It was African in origin but Egyptian in tradition and religious belief. There was a pharaonic-style court; Amon-Ra was worshipped in a magnificent temple built to his glory near Gebal Barkal, a sacred mountain near the Fourth Cataract, and the Kushite kings styled themselves with pharaonic titles.

The Kushite king Piankhy finally saw it as his duty to liberate Egypt from what he considered to be the forces of barbarism and to restore the ancient culture. He marched northwards with a strong army and presented himself to the people of Egypt as a true pharaoh. In fact, during the 25th Dynasty (750–656 BC), Piankhy and his descendants did much to restore to Egypt some of its earlier greatness. Shabako was the first Kushite king of a united Upper and Lower Egypt, and in his reign ancient texts were copied and temples restored. How long a Kushite king might have remained on the throne of Egypt we cannot say. For the Assyrian army marched on the Delta 671 BC, and in the face of their military might, the Kushites were driven back to their own land.

Apart from a short-lived revival in the 26th Dynasty, Egypt's great civilisation was on the decline. But far to the south, the Kushite kingdom prospered. Around 600 BC the leaders decided to move their capital from Napata to Meroe (Shendi). In the fertile bend in the river, free from invasion, well-placed for trade, rich in iron ore and in wood for iron-smelting, they developed a culture that was at once a continuation of the Egyptian-influenced Napatan culture and a totally individual African culture. (More will soon be known of this civilization, for the Meroitic script, a corruption of the hieroglyphic, is at last on its way to decipherment.)

Egypt succumbed to two Persian invasions while the Meroitic Empire spread northwards. Egypt was conquered by Alexander the Great, and by the reign of Ptolemy IV (181 BC), a Meroitic king, Argamanic, controlled the Nile to within sight of Elephantine.

When the Romans took over Egypt (30 BC), they signed a treaty with the Meroites, turning all Lower Nubia into a buffer zone. Yet, despite their alliance, there is evidence of conflict between the proud and independent Meroites and the Roman garrisons. On one occasion the Meroites defeated Caesar's soldiers and actually occupied Aswan. In retaliation, however, the Roman army drove them back to their own land. Their civilization prospered until the middle of the fourth century AD.

With the departure of the Meroitic army, the Nubians were able to enjoy some prosperity once again. During the Roman period, the temple of Kalabsha, dedicated to the Nubian god Mandolis, was completed; and other temples were built at Debod, Dendur and Dakka. Worship of the ancient gods of Egypt in the land of Nubia lingered on until the sixth century, long after Egypt had been converted to Christianity.

The Rescued Monuments of Nubia

Nubia, the beautiful austere land that once linked Egypt and black Africa, now lies beneath the world's largest man-made lake. Gone forever are the neat domed houses of the Nubian people, the unique façades of which were decorated with coloured plates. Their villages, places of worship and burial grounds were all doomed to destruction when plans for the building of the High Dam went ahead in 1960. The entire population of nearly 100,000 people faced the sorrowful but inevitable fact that they would have to be uprooted and resettled elsewhere.

The people of Egyptian Nubia, some 50,000 in number, started a new life at Kom Ombo, about fifty miles downstream from the High Dam. The Upper Nubians were taken to the eastern part of the Sudan to a place called Kashm el-Girba. By 1971 Nubia had passed into history.

Yet, ironically, it is due to its disappearance that more is now known about Nubia than most archaeological sites, even in Luxor. During the decade when the High Dam was being built, before the waters began to rise, the entire area was subjected to studies on a scale never before witnessed. Engineers, architects, photographers, artists, restorers, archaeologists, anthropologists, social scientists and historians came to study, photograph, document and salvage

Sluices of the High Dam

whatever they could in the most ambitious salvage operation ever undertaken.

The international campaign to save the monuments of Nubia was sponsored by the Egyptian and Sudanese governments and UNESCO in 1960. Over a period of two decades, no less than twenty-three temples and shrines were saved. Some monuments were partially saved (the temples of **Gerf Hussein** and **Aksha**); one was lifted as a unit of 800 tons, put on rails and dragged up a hill to safety (temple of **Amada**); several were dismantled in the reverse process used to build them; that is to say, they were completely filled and surrounded with sand; the inscribed blocks were then lifted off the top of the temple. As each layer was removed the sand was lowered to reveal the next layer. After transportation to another site, the temples were rebuilt (the temple of Hatshepsut from **Buhen**, weighing 600 tons, was thus transported to the new Sudanese Museum at Khartoum in 59 cases aboard 28 trucks). A much more challenging project was the saving of the beautiful monuments of the **Island of Philae** (page 187), and the project at **Abu Simbel** represents one of the most outstanding feats of civil engineering in our times.

PLAN TO SAVE THE TEMPLES OF ABU SIMBEL

There are two temples at Abu Simbel: the Great Temple of Ramses II and the small temple of Nefertari, his Great Royal Wife. Both were excavated out of the solid rock of a mountain. They could not, therefore, be dismantled, transported and re-erected elsewhere, as with other temples. Here was a formidable challenge. The Temple of Ramses II was the largest and one of the most magnificent monuments of the ancient world, and Egypt launched an appeal to UNESCO.

The response was immediate. Countries from all over the world offered aid, both technical and financial. Many different proposals were presented and studied. Finally, in 1960, a project presented by a Stockholm Company of Consulting Engineers was chosen as the most feasible and least costly. The basic idea of the 'VBB' Scheme, as it came to be known, was literally to saw the temple into transportable blocks and place them safely above the water level until they could be rebuilt sixty-four metres above their original site.

An international consortium of contractors, working alongside archaeologists, laid out a plan of action. The first stage was the construction of a coffer-dam. This was necessary so that work on sectionalizing the temples could continue even after the summer of 1964, when the old course of the Nile was closed and the water level began to rise.

The sawing of the temple into over a thousand transportable pieces, some weighing as much as fifteen tons, was no easy task. Experiments were made with different techniques. Decisions had to be made on where the divisions should be made. Cranes carefully lifted each separate block. After hauling it to a storage site, it was pivotted to a huge piece of concrete for stability and then treated with resin for protection.

Meanwhile the new site, on the top of the mountain, was being levelled with the aid of drills operated by compressed air. Explosives could not be used for fear of damaging the temples. Studies were then made on the bedrock to ensure that it could support the enormous weight of rock it was destined to bear forever; not the reconstructed temples alone, but also the great reinforced concrete dome that would cover it and support the weight of the reconstructed mountain.

The project was completed in December 1968. When approached from the front, the temples of Abu Simbel have their same orientation and setting. It was decided, however, that the artificial hill reconstructed over the temple should not be disguised from the rear. As the visitor approaches the site from the airport, it is the smoothed and ridged rock-fill over the dome that can be seen.

DESCRIPTION

The Great Temple of Ramses II
There are few monuments of ancient Egypt that have been so frequently described as this great temple of Ramses II at Abu Simbel. From the time of its opening by the Italian Giovanni Belzoni in 1817 to the present-day, when it has become world-famous for having been salvaged from the rising waters of the Nile, it has fascinated all who see it.

Ramses II chose a site some 280 kilometres south of Aswan. Though the temple is primarily dedicated to Amon-Ra of Thebes and Ra-Harakhte of Heliopolis, it was also designed as a memorial to Ramses' vanity, for it is dedicated also to the deified Ramses II himself.

Ramses II was an indefatigable builder, and he repeated the theme of the battle he fought at Kadesh on the Orontes river in Syria

Great Temple of Ramses II at Abu Simbel

in the fifth year of his reign on all his monuments. His enemy was the Hittite King Muwattalish and a coalition of neighbouring chiefs. Far from the great victory he recorded, Ramses barely snatched it from humiliating defeat by the timely arrival of two Egyptian divisions: one from Heliopolis under the banner of Ra-Harakhte and the other from Memphis under the banner of Ptah. Ramses had command of the forward division from Luxor, under the banner of Amon-Ra.

The **Façade** of the temple, which is actually the cliff face hewn in imitation of a pylon, is crowned by a frieze of baboons. It rises to a height of 32 metres. The width at the base is 35 metres and 32 metres at the top. Dominating the façade are four seated statues of a youthful Ramses II. They loom in huge dimension to some 20 metres, and are believed to be the same size as the broken granite colossus in the Ramesseum. Ramses sits with his hands on his knees. His countenance is mild. On his chest and upper arm are oblong 'cartouches' bearing his name. On his forehead is the sacred uraeus. cobra, symbol of kingship. He wears the double crown of Upper and Lower Egypt. According to the records, Ramses, who ruled for 67 years, was married to at least three legitimate wives and had no fewer than 170 children. Some members of the royal family are shown with him. To the left of the second colossus (b) is Ramses' mother.

To the right is Nefertari, his most beloved wife. Between his legs are royal relatives.

On each side of the right-hand colossi (c) and (d) are representations of two Nile-gods binding the floral symbols of the Two Lands, the papyrus and the lotus, around the hieroglyphic symbol for 'Unite'. Below is a row of captives: Nubian prisoners to the south and Syrians to the north.

Above the entrance, standing in a niche, is the hawk-headed Ra-Harakhte, worshipped on either side by Ramses II, who presents tiny statuettes of Maat, goddess of Truth.

A passage leads to the **Courtyard Hall** (1), 18 metres long, 16 metres wide and 8 metres high. Eight enormous statues of the King stand in a double row, facing each other, against a corresponding number of square pillars. He is represented in Osirian form with crook and flail. The ceiling is adorned with flying vultures (central aisle) and with stars and the names and titles of the king (side aisles).

The walls teem with beautifully painted reliefs. Most are religious ceremonies and battle scenes. The style is bolder (though not superior) to other monuments. On each side of the entrance (e)

GREAT TEMPLE OF RAMSES II AT ABU SIMBEL
Plan 31

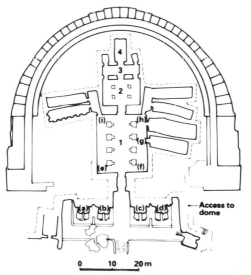

0   10   20 m

and (f) are vividly coloured reliefs that show Ramses clasping his enemies by the hair and smiting them with a club. He performs this act in the presence of Amon-Ra, who hands him a curved sword of victory at (e), and the hawk-headed Ra-Harakhte at (f). In fact, this division of the temple between Amon-Ra and Ra-Harakhte continues throughout its entire length. Most of the reliefs of the former are on the south side (left) of the temple, and those of Ra-Harakhte are to the north (right).

Both sides of the hall are decorated with scenes of a military nature. The **Great Battle Scene** is on the northern wall (g). It covers an area of 18 metres in length and 8 metres in height. It is one of the most extraordinary and detailed reliefs to be found in the Nile Valley. There are over 1100 figures depicted and the entire wall space from the ceiling to the bedrock is filled with activity: the march of the Egyptian army with its infantry and charioteers, hand-to-hand combat, the flight of the vanquished, prisoners, slain, wounded and drowning enemy. There are overturned chariots, riderless horses and farmers anxiously driving their cattle into the hills. There are scenes of camp life and inspection of officers. Here in a single mural is all the pomp and circumstance of war.

With their traditional stress on balance and symmetry, the artists have separated the wall into registers. Between the war scenes above and the Egyptian army below, is a frieze of charging chariots at full gallop. On the lower half of the wall, between the two doors (1), are scenes of Egyptian camp life. The camp is square and enclosed by a stockade of soldiers' shields. The royal tent is shown, and at the centre of the camp is Ramses' pet lion that is cared for by a keeper. Horses are being fed in rows from a common manger. Some wait impatiently pawing the ground. Others lie down. Some are being harnessed. One horse scampers around the enclosure. One makes off dragging an empty chariot, pursued by a couple of grooms. There are joints of meat (in the corner) and a tripod brazier. Soldiers eat from a common bowl as they crouch on their heels. One officer is

**Battle of Kadesh
(Abu Simbel)**

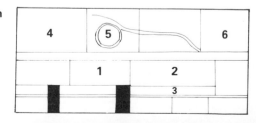

having his wounded foot dressed by a doctor. Another sits with his head resting on his hand. Hurrying towards him is a soldier bringing news of the battle.

To the right (2) the seated Ramses holds a council of war with his officers. In the lower register (3) two spies are being interrogated. According to textual evidence, these two men of the *Shasu* tribe came into the Egyptian camp then situated in the land of *Tchal*, not far from Kadesh. They claimed to have been sent by their chiefs to inform Ramses that the Hittites wished to come to terms with the Egyptian army. They declared that the enemy were yet some distance away and afraid to make contact. The two men were, in fact, sent by the Hittite leaders with false information in order to establish the exact position of the Egyptian army. At that very moment, the enemy was actually drawn up in full battle array behind Kadesh. No sooner had the men been dismissed than an Egyptian scout requested urgent presence with the king and brought the two spies with him. They finally admitted that the chief of Kheta was encamped behind Kadesh with soldiers and chariots ready to strike. Naturally Ramses blamed his own intelligence for neglect of duty, and after admitting their fault, the Egyptian army made immediate preparation to march on Kadesh.

The clash of arms is depicted on the upper reaches of the wall, where the river Orontes winds through the picture and almost surrounds the beseiged city. Commanding the scene is Ramses II in a pitched battle (4). Watching the scene from the strongly defended fortress of Kadesh (5) are some of the enemy who peer from the embattlements. Ramses stands undaunted in his chariot surrounded by the enemy. With the sure confidence of a warrior, he whips up his horses and dashes into the Hittite ranks, launching arrows at them and crushing many beneath the wheels of his chariot. Among the slain and the fallen are some who beg for mercy.

So wonderful was his bravery that a poem composed by Pen-ta-urt was inscribed on the walls of many of the temples Ramses built. It recorded for posterity how the great pharaoh, in full armour and mounted on his chariot, drove into battle with a 'growl like that of his father Montu, Lord of Thebes'. How, suddenly finding himself completely surrounded and cut off from his own troops, Ramses called on the name of Amon-Ra, whipped up his horses and slaughtered the enemy until some fell 'in great heaps on the ground' while others fell one over the other into the waters of the Orontes. Quite alone and with not one of his infantry to help him, Ramses thus succeeded in forcing his way through the enemy ranks. On the extreme right (6) the king, still in his chariot, inspects his officers, as they count the severed hands of the enemy and bring in fettered prisoners.

The walls to the rear of the hall show Egyptians leading rows of captive Hittites towards Ra-Harakhte and his own deified figure at (h); rows of captive Nubians are presented to Amon-Ra, Ramses, as a deity, and Mut at (i). (*The large chambers leading off the Hall were probably storerooms; the reliefs are of inferior quality*).

The **Hypostyle Hall** (2) has four supporting square pillars. The reliefs are of offerings made by Ramses II to the various gods, one of which is the deified Ramses II himself, and various ritual scenes that show the sacred barge of Amon-Ra and accompanying priests. Following the Hypostyle Hall is an ante-chamber (3) and the Sanctuary.

The **Sanctuary** (4) contains four seated statues: Ptah, Amon-Ra, the deified Ramses II, and Ra-Harakhte. The temple is so oriented on an east-west axis that the rising sun sends its rays to strike the rear wall of the sanctuary, 47 metres back from the entrance, or 61 metres inside the mountain surface. At certain times of the year the rising sun illuminates the sanctuary and shines on the four seated statues. Much has been said about this phenomenon; though in fact even when the sun's rays pass through all the entrances of the chambers, the sanctuary wall and the four statues are never fully illuminated. Twice a year, however, for 25 days after the autumnal equinox of September 23, and 25 days before the vernal equinox of March 20, the axis of the temple enables the statues to be illuminated – though never more than two at a time. The most that can be seen is on February 26th and October 18th when the sun shines on the statues of Amon-Ra and Ramses, with the light touching the sides of the flanking statues of Ptah (on the left) and Ra-Harakhte (on the right).

The Great Dome Access is gained via a stairway to the right of the temple that leads to a gallery, from which this impressive, weighty, concrete shrine can be seen from the inside. It was designed to relieve the temple structure below from the very heavy load of the overlying rock walls and rockfill and also to make possible inspection and repair (if necessary) from the rear.

It represents a unique technological achievement. Owing to its size and the complex nature of its load, it was necessary to carry out measurements of stress, strain and deformation, in order to check the behaviour and the safety of the structure. Also, to make calculations to evaluate its long-term behaviour and durability.

The height of the dome is 25 metres and the cylindrical part has a

TEMPLE OF NEFERTARI AT ABU SIMBEL Plan 32

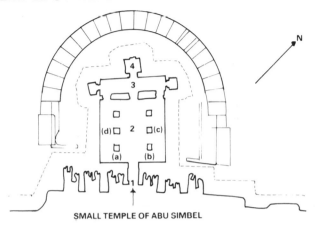

SMALL TEMPLE OF ABU SIMBEL

free span of some 60 metres. This single span is destined to bear a load of about 100,000 metric tons, and its durability must at least match that of the temple it shelters!

Temple of Nefertari
Nefertari, or Beautiful Companion, was the first and most beloved of the wives of Ramses II. Indeed, her form is slim and graceful, and she is extremely fair. Since her magnificent tomb in the Valley of the Queens at Luxor is closed to the general public, we are fortunate that we can see her depicted in her temple at Abu Simbel. It lies to the north of the great temple of Ramses II and is dedicated to Nefertari and to the goddess Hathor.

The terrace (1) leads to the sloping façade that provides the frame for six recesses, three on each side of the central doorway. Within each there are standing figures: four of the king and two of the queen. They appear to be walking forward with spirited strides. Ramses wears an elaborate crown of plumes and horns. On Nefertari's head are plumes and the sun disc. At their sides are small figures of their children – the princesses beside Nefertari and the princes beside Ramses.

The legend of the love of Ramses for his wife is enumerated along with his titles: 'Ramses, strong in *Maat* (Truth), beloved of Amon, made this divine abode for his royal wife, Nefertari, whom he loves'.

Throughout the temple, on pillar and wall, and even in the sanctuary, the names of the royal couple are linked in their shared dedication to the goddess Hathor.

The buttressed sloping projections between the figures on the façade bear hieroglyphic votive inscriptions. At the centre of the broadest, central section is the doorway leading to the Hypostyle Hall (2), a traverse chamber (3) and the sanctuary (4). The thickness of the doorway shows Ramses before Hathor, to the south, and Nefertari before Isis, to the north; Isis makes a gesture as though to crown her.

The Hypostyle Hall (2) has six pillars decorated on the front with sistra – the musical instrument associated with the goddess Hathor – and with the heads of Hathor. Behind are representations of Ramses, Nefertari and various deities. The reliefs on the entrance walls (a) and (b) have fine representations of Ramses, accompanied by Nefertari, smiting a Libyan in the presence of Ra-Harakhte, and a Nubian in the presence of Amon-Ra respectively. The side walls have similar offering scenes. At (c) Ramses offers food to Ptah and also stands in front of the ram-headed Harshef. Nefertari makes offerings to Hathor. And Ramses offers wine to Ra-Harakhte. At (d) Ramses stands before Hathor. Ramses is blessed by Horus and Set of Nubt. Nefertari stands before Anukis. And Ramses presents an image of *Maat* to Amon. On the rear walls are Nefertari and Hathor (to the right) and Nefertari and Mut (to the left). Mut was the wife of Amon-Ra and, like Hathor, a mother figure.

The traverse chamber (3) is adjoined by two unfinished chambers, to the right and left. Over the doorways, however, are reliefs of Hathor the sacred cow in a marsh, which are worth noting. In one case, Hathor is being worshipped by Ramses and in the other by Nefertari.

The sanctuary (4) has a recess to the rear, and the roof is supported by sistra. A representation of Hathor in the form of a cow protecting the king (who appears below her head) is a fine relief. On the right-hand wall Nefertari offers incense to Mut and Hathor. On the left the king pours a libation over his own image and also that of his wife.

Monuments of Nubia
reconstructed near the High Dam (Aswan)

The site chosen for the reconstruction of four monuments from Nubia, on the western bank of the Nile, was supposed to remain as a part of the mainland. The waters of the High Dam Lake, however, have risen higher than expected, and now surround the site. This makes it unapproachable except by launch via the High Dam port, and permission to visit the site is a lengthy affair. It is hoped that the plans to build a bridge and a new road will go ahead soon, as the site is well worth seeing.

Apart from the Temple of Kalabsha, which is the largest on the site, are the Temple of Beit el Wali, the delightful Kiosk of Kertassi, some blocks with painted reliefs from the Ramesside era, extracted from the rock-hewn Temple of Gerf Hussein, and some pre-dynastic rock drawings of elephants, saved before the inundation of Nubia. The latter (the blocks from Gerf Hussein, which await reconstruction, and the rock drawings) unfortunately lie un-protected in the searing heat of Aswan.

Temple of Kalabsha

This was one of the largest free-standing temples of Nubia, over 76 metres long and 22 metres wide. It has been saved by the Federal Republic of Germany from the flooding. Twenty thousand tons of stone were transported and the temple was re-erected fifteen kilometres south of Aswan, close beside the High Dam. The whole project took eighteen months and is another feat of salvage archaeology.

While dismantling the temple, some of the inscribed and decorated stones in the foundations proved to have been reused from earlier monuments: a Ptolemaic shrine, and a gateway attached to it. The great reconstructed gateway was given to the Federal Republic of Germany in recognition of their contribution to the Nubian campaign (it is now in the Egyptian Museum in West Berlin); the shrine has been rebuilt on the south end of Elephantine island.

This temple is built entirely of Nubian sandstone and is dedicated to the Nubian god Merul (Greek Mandolis) a rough equivalent of the Egyptian Osiris. It was probably started by Thutmose III and added to by his son, Amenhotep II, whose reliefs have survived. During the Ptolemaic period, major repairs were carried out, and columns of the Ptolemaic period stand in the forecourt. Many of the reliefs and inscriptions date to the Roman period. With the introduction of Christianity the temple was converted into a church.

142

TEMPLE OF KALABSHA Plan 33

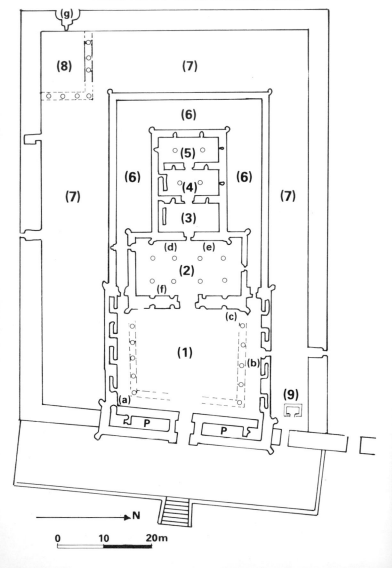

0   10   20m

Temple of Kalabsha (reconstructed near the High Dam)

The **Entrance Pylon** (P) is at a slight angle to the main temple. It is approached from a terrace and is unadorned, apart from the representations of deities in the thickness of the doorway and grooves for the flag-staffs. The top of the pylon can be mounted via a stairway on the inside of the left-hand pylon (a).

The Court (1) was surrounded on three sides by colonnades of richly adorned floral capitals. On each side of the court four tiny chambers have been constructed within the wall. A doorway to the right (b) leads to the passage that surrounds the temple (7) and a shrine (8).

To the rear of the court is a façade of imposing columns joined by walls leading to the hypostyle hall. The walls are decorated. The two to the left bear representations of Thoth and Horus, who anoint the king, and a representation of the seated Harsiesis. The first wall to the right bears the celebrated decree of Aurelius, military overseer of Ombos and Elephantine (*c*. AD 248). It is written in Greek and orders the owners of pigs to remove their animals from the temple.

On the second column to the right are two more Greek inscriptions, and between them is a long inscription in Meroitic script; this was the last modification of the cursive hieroglyphics adapted to the native language.

The last inscription in the temple may be found in the right-hand corner of the façade (c). It dates to the latter half of the sixth century and records that the Blemmys were defeated by Silko, king of Nubia and Ethiopia (Kush was known as Ethiopia in Graeco-Roman times).

The Hypostyle Hall (2) has twelve columns, the first four united by screen walls. All the columns have elaborate floral decorations. The reliefs to the rear (at d), show a Ptolemaic pharaoh making offerings of land to Isis, Mandolis and another deity with a shield. To the right (e) Amenhotep II, the original founder of the temple, is depicted offering a libation to Min and Mandolis. On the screen wall to the left of the entrance (f) is an interesting painting dating to the Christian era; it shows the damned in a fiery furnace being handed a sword by an angel.

The chambers to the rear (3), (4) and (5) have excellently preserved reliefs in colour – so bright as to be considered garish. On the base of the walls of the first chamber is a procession of Nile-gods being led by the pharaoh, with offerings for Mandolis, Osiris, Isis and other deities. A stairway inside the left-hand wall leads to the roof of the third chamber (5).

The second chamber (4) shows Roman emperors before the gods. The stairway from this chamber leads to the top of the girdle wall that leads to a tiny two-roomed shrine with a crypt (g), which was formed in the thickness of the wall.

The sanctuary is decorated with reliefs, also well preserved, but of inferior artistic execution. It is interesting to see the Nubian type becoming manifest, even in the physionomies of the pharaohs and the headdresses and costumes of the deities. These reliefs in a temple in Nubia, showing Isis and Horus, the most loved of deities, depicted with dark faces, are curious.

The passage surrounding the inner chambers (6), which is approached from the court (1), contains representations of Roman emperors before the deities.

In the outer passage (7), which was built against the rock in the temple's original setting in Nubia, there was a shrine (perhaps a Birth House) at the left-hand corner (8), and another well-preserved shrine (9) in the north-eastern angle, both believed to date from Ptolemaic times; they have not been rebuilt in Kalabsha Temple, but reconstructed on the south of the Island of Elephantine.

Near the temple of Kalabsha, lying to the south, are some **rock inscriptions**, which were also saved before the inundation of Nubia.

Temple of Beit el Wali

This is another of Ramses II's rock-hewn temples of Nubia, built in honour of Amon-Ra, the Horuses of Nubia and the gods of the cataracts. It was originally situated to the north of Kalabsha (see page 126) and has been moved to a site close to Kalabsha Temple, now near the High Dam at Aswan by a Polish archaeological team, financed by a joint Oriental Institute of Chicago/Swiss Institute of Cairo project.

This is a small temple, comprising an outer courtyard (later converted into a church) a hypostyle hall and a sanctuary. The reliefs of the inner temple are well preserved, and there are some interesting scenes of the military campaign in Upper Nubia (bordering Kush), in the outer court, showing scenes of life in Kush.

On the *left-hand* wall of the outer court, Ramses II is depicted in his chariot. With his usual bravado he charges the enemy who flee before him. He is accompanied by his two sons, each of whom has his own chariot and chariot driver. The Kushites are armed with bows and arrows. The men, with their women and children, escape to their camp that is situated among the *dom* palm-trees. One woman carries a child in a basket held to her back by a strap round the forehead. Another, who is cooking, looks up in terror to see the Egyptians approaching.

Towards the rear of this wall, Ramses, with his sons and noblemen, sits beneath a canopy while the Kushites bring him tribute. In the upper register are bags of precious objects, gold rings, bows, animal skins, shields, furniture including an ornamented chair, elephant tusks, and animals, including a lion and gazelles. In the lower register are prisoners, animals (monkeys, a leopard and giraffe), and women with their children.

On the *right-hand* wall of the outer court are scenes of Ramses' campaigns in Asia and Libya. They depict the usual themes of attacking the enemy fortress and Ramses holding a group of Syrian captives by the hair while he smites them with a raised axe. In another scene he puts a kneeling figure of a Libyan to death while his pet lion takes a bite out of the doomed man's heel.

Scenes of foreign campaigns depicted in a Nubian temple would appear to be designed to show the native peoples that Ramses was powerful from one end of the empire to the other. He is shown with Egyptian noblemen and princes, bowing slightly to him in respect.

Three doorways to the rear of the court lead into the hypostyle hall, which has two stout fluted columns supporting the roof. Over the central doorway is the figure of Ramses in front of Amon-Ra.

Other scenes in the hall are of conquests and offerings. The doorway to the rear, leading to the sanctuary, had niches for three seated figures on either side. All were badly damaged, but probably represented Ramses between his fellow gods.

The colouring and reliefs of the rock-hewn sanctuary are well preserved. The badly damaged statues in a niche to the rear probably represented Ramses between two deities. Moving clockwise from the doorway, they show:

Ramses II is being embraced by Satis and suckled by Isis. On the *left-hand* wall he makes offerings to Horus and Amon-Ra. On the rear wall (on the sides of the niche) are figures of Min and Ptah. The *right-hand* wall shows Ramses suckled by Anukis, goddess of Elephantine. Towards the entrance doorway is a defaced figure of Ramses embraced by Miket.

Kiosk of Kertassi
This tiny structure, only about 25 feet square and dedicated to two Nubian deities, once stood on a rocky hill not far from the site used for quarrying Nubian sandstone. Its delicate columns rising against the sky made it a landmark of the area. In its original position it faced north and its entrance was flanked by two Hathor-columns. It has now been re-erected at a site near the High Dam.

THE MONUMENTS SAVED FROM EGYPTIAN NUBIA
(See enlarged section of Plan (page 126) for original sites.)

Philae	All the monuments, including the magnificent Temple of Isis, have now been reconstructed on the neighbouring Island of Agilkai (page 183).
Debod	A Graeco-Roman temple that was dismantled and transported to Madrid now stands on a cliff with an artificial channel in front of it.
Kertassi	A Graeco-Roman kiosk that has been re-erected on the western bank of the Nile near the High Dam (see above).

Tafa	A Graeco-Roman temple that now stands in a courtyard of the Museum in Leiden.
Beit el Wali	A rock temple hewn out of a cliff by Ramses II at Kalabsha has been moved to a site near the High Dam (page 145).
Kalabsha	This temple, in honour of the Nubian god Mandolis, has been re-erected near the High Dam (near the Kiosk of Kertassi) (page 146). Reused blocks of a gateway and a shrine were found in the foundations of the temple. The former now stands in the Museum of the Federal Republic of Germany; the latter has been rebuilt on the Island of Elephantine.
Dendur	This Graeco-Roman temple now stands in a special hall in the Metropolitan Museum in New York.
Dakka	An 18th Dynasty temple, rebuilt in the Kushite Period and dedicated to Osiris, Isis and Horus, has been moved to a site at Wadi es-Sebua in Nubia.
Maharraka	A Graeco-Roman temple transported to a site at Wadi es-Sebua in Nubia.
Sebua	A fine temple built by Ramses II in honour of Amon-Ra and Ra-Harakhte and converted into a church in the Christian period. It contains frescoes over the original reliefs. It was dismantled and moved to higher ground in a joint ARE/US/French/Swiss project. The Christian inscriptions were preserved by a team of Yugoslav archaeologists.
Amada	An 18th Dynasty temple transported as a unit of 800 tons on rail by the French Government. Much of the original relief was preserved due to its being covered with stucco and repainted in the Christian era.
Derr	A temple built by Ramses II in honour of Ra, removed to a site at Amada.
Ellessya	A small 18th Dynasty temple started by Thutmose III. It now stands in the Egyptian Museum in Turin.
Abu Simbel	The Great Temple of Ramses II and the smaller Temple of Nefertari have been rebuilt atop the mountain (page 133).

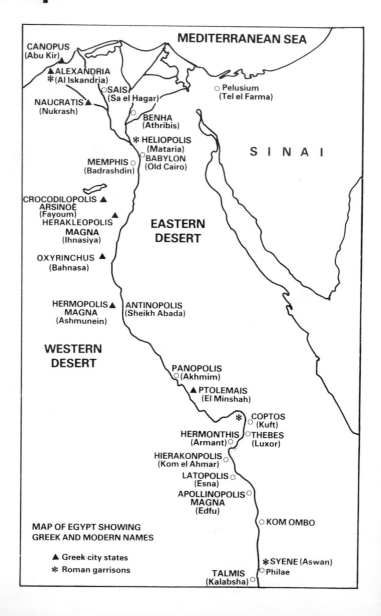

MAP OF EGYPT SHOWING
GREEK AND MODERN NAMES

▲ Greek city states

✳ Roman garrisons

PART II

CHAPTER 6   GRAECO-ROMAN PERIOD
(332 BC–AD 395)

BACKGROUND

The Graeco-Roman period covers some six centuries and may be divided into two periods: the **Ptolemaic Period** (332–30 BC), when Egypt lost its independent status after Alexander the Great's conquest; following his death his empire was divided, and Egypt fell to the share of Ptolemy I Soter (Saviour). He and his successors were known as the Ptolemies, and during their rule, Egypt became, once more, the seat of a powerful kingdom. Egypt of the Ptolemies fell under the growing influence of Rome and finally became a province of the empire. During the **Roman Period** (30 BC–AD 395), an effort was made to maintain the appearance of a national state, but Egypt was no more than a dependant of Rome. Hard-pressed to meet the demand for grain, and persecuted by the Romans, many Egyptians sought refuge in a life of asceticism, founding the monastic way of life (Chapter 8).

Ptolemaic Egypt (332–30 BC)
When Alexander marched on Egypt, the Egyptians had no reason to fear that this would be the beginning of the end of their status as an independent nation. Alexander promised to liberate them, and they put their full trust in him. Their shared hostility to the Persians bound them together; Alexander's army had just defeated the Persian army in Asia, and Egypt's patience was being sorely tried by a second occupation. Moreover, the Egyptians did not need to be reminded that when Athens was fighting its own weary wars with Sparta, the Greeks had despatched a fleet of two hundred ships (all

lost) to help Egypt revolt against their shared long-time enemy. A common antagonist breeds understanding, and the welcome of Alexander was genuine. The Egyptians did indeed regard him as a deliverer.

What they may have failed to realise was that, with the single exception of Egypt, Persian power had been suppressed and that Alexander, who had already made himself master of the disunited Greek world, planned to join Egypt to his already widely extended empire.

Alexander made his way to thickly-populated Memphis. There he made an offering at the shrine of the sacred Apis bull – a gesture much appreciated by the Egyptians. Then he lost no time in travelling to Siwa Oasis to consult the famous oracle of Amon-Ra. When he emerged from the sacred sanctuary, he announced that the statue of the god had, by inclination of the head, indicated his acceptance of leadership. He was forthwith hailed by the priests as the 'son of Amon'.

Before he left Egypt, Alexander laid down the basic plans for its government. In the important provinces he appointed local governors from among Egyptian nobles. He made provision for the collection of taxes under his financial superintendent, and he established a small standing army under his general Ptolemy. He also laid out the plans for his great city and seaport, Alexandria, so situated as to facilitate the flow of Egypt's surplus resources to the archipelago and also to intercept all trade with Africa and Asia.

When Alexander met his untimely death of a fever at Babylon, the great Macedonian Empire declined. Egypt was held by Ptolemy, who gradually took over leadership, first as Satrap*, then Governor and, finally, in 305 BC, as King. During the three centuries of the Ptolemaic Period that followed, Egypt became once more the most prosperous, rich and powerful state in the world.

The Ptolemies played a dual role in Egypt. They conducted themselves as both Greeks and as pharaohs. The two were separate and polarised roles. As Greeks they resided in Alexandria, a predominantly Greek capital, where there was a Greek senate, gymnasium, and amphitheatre. The Museum and Library were planned on Athenian models, and youngsters were raised on a literary diet of Homer and the Greek classics. The Ptolemies were astute businessmen, and their aim was, of course, mastery of the Mediterranean world. Their fleet was manned by Greek mercenary troops, who were accommodated on large tracts of land reclaimed in the Fayoum, a fertile depression south of the apex of the Delta. The

Ptolemies saw themselves as landowners and Egypt as a mighty farm.

The Greek states, however, had had no organisation like that of Egypt for the assessment and collection of taxes, and the Ptolemies were quick to realize the benefits of leaving to trained Egyptians the task that they had carried on for thousands of years. In order to do this they reorganised the old Egyptian divisions of the country into different provinces, called 'nomes', under a governor, whom they designated 'nomarch'. To please the Egyptians further and show that they were governed, not by foreigners, but by kings more traditional even than the ancient pharaohs themselves, the Ptolemies decided to conciliate the priesthoods throughout the country.

Herein lay the second role of the Ptolemaic kings: that of legitimate pharaohs. As 'heirs' of the ancient kings of Egypt, they lavished revenues on some of the priesthoods for the upkeep of temples or exempted them from taxes. Then, like the ancient pharaohs, they assumed religious office and journeyed up the Nile to make offerings at these temples. Thus giving prestige to the local priests and entrusting nomarchs with the task of tax collection and control of revenue, they acquired the loyalty and devotion of the Egyptian people.

A Ptolemaic king in the traditional garb making offerings

Of course, public worship of political leadership was a feature of the central religious organisation that had long existed in Egypt, and the Ptolemies were ready to accept symbolic acts of homage, if it pleased the local population. Local artisans tackled the task of temple construction and reconstruction with vigour. The temples were built on Egyptian plans and decorated by Egyptian craftsmen, depicting the Ptolemaic kings on the walls in the manner of the ancient pharaohs; they were duly inscribed with pharaonic titles and ranks in the symbolic language of which the Ptolemies themselves had no knowledge. Rare are the representations of them dressed in Greek robes and not as Egyptian pharaohs.

Some of the most beautiful temples in the Nile valley date from the Ptolemaic period. Such monuments as those found at Dendera, Edfu, Kom Ombo and on the island of Philae are dignified though ornate. They show fine architectural proportions, although the figures and inscriptions themselves do not compare with the masterly executions from the tombs of the Old Kingdom at Sakkara or the temples of the New Kingdom.

It is worthy of note, however, that the sites chosen by the Ptolemies were for their strategic position as well as for the ancient tradition. Edfu, for example, was an ancient depot for caravans from Kharga Oasis to the west and from the Red Sea coast. Esna had been a centre for local commerce from earliest times. Kom Ombo, situated on a hill, commanded the trade routes to Nubia, and the temples on the Nubian frontier (Philae, Kalabsha, Debod, Taffa and Dendur) were clearly of strategic importance. Each was a focus of commerce.

Thus, we have Alexandria, a Greek capital, which became the seat of learning where the framers of science, philosophy, poetry and art flocked. On the other hand we have the marvellous fertile land of Egypt, with nomarchs facilitating the collection of taxes in order to fulfill the economic needs of the Greek capital. It is significant that, apart from a small number of priestly literates, Egyptian citizenship was not encouraged at Alexandria. But neither, it should be noted, were Egyptians ever slaves in the Ptolemaic court. Slaves were usually Asiatic.

The reputation of Egypt as a land of wonders was widespread on the Greek mainland long before the occupation, and the Greeks held the Egyptian culture in reverence. Traders from the Nile valley, from Phoenicia and from Asia had long talked of the strange gods and of the wonderful temples. When Herodotus travelled to the Nile valley during the first Persian occupation (445 BC), he took back to

Greece stories that made a lasting impression on the people; though Greek scholars had traced political events to earthly causes and had received enthusiastic approval among the educated classes, Herodotus' tales of the will of the gods, as prophesied in divine oracles and 'sacred mysteries' (in fact they were traditional dramas), had greater appeal with the masses. Hordes of soldiers, merchants, craftsmen, businessmen, beggar-priests and soothsayers, who had once filed in solemn procession along the roads leading to Delphi or had participated in the mysteries of Eleusis, now took refuge in the Nile valley, where they came for the strange and the mystical.

The Ptolemies saw the need to create a national god that would be equally acceptable to the Egyptians as to the cult-seekers of the Greek world. Egypt's most beloved god, Osiris, was identified with their own invented god Serapis and declared to be the official god. Of course, Osiris, as god of the underworld, became one with Hades (Pluto) of the underworld. The cult of Isis was also promoted and Hellenised; as the beloved wife of Osiris and mother of Horus, she was identified with the earth-mother Demeter.

To cater for the vast Egyptian, Greek and Macedonian masses, the Ptolemies identified Egypt's deities with deities of the Greek islands and the Asian mainland: Egypt's Amon-Ra, king of the Gods, was identified with Zeus, supreme god of Olympus; Amon's wife, Mut, was identified with Hera, Queen of the Sky. The Egyptian Horus was easily identified with Apollo, both being regarded as Sun-gods; Thoth, the Egyptian god of wisdom, who invented writing, was associated with Hermes, messenger of Zeus. A common culture to embrace a whole range of cultural interests, rites and mysteries was created that provided for the widest possible audience.

Both Greek and Egyptian could worship his own god under a Greek or an Egyptian name in the same temple. Though annual festivals were still geared to the seasons and were joyous if solemn affairs, the 'initiation mysteries' and the mysterious 'stunts' (like the claim that the statue of Amon at Siwa nodded in approval of Alexander's kingship) greatly appealed to the masses. And the priests, who claimed a knowledge of the special secrets of oracles, aroused awe in the curious spectator and evoked responsive faith in the believer.

During the Ptolemaic period, public records of the activities of the pharaohs, as well as details of national and religious feasts – Greek and Egyptian – were presented to the public. Consequently, such texts as those inscribed on the famous Rosetta Stone (which provided the key to the deciphering of hieroglyphics) and the Decree of Canopus (which survives in three copies) bore two forms of the Egyptian script, hieroglyphics and its later development, demotic, along with a Greek translation. They were copied on stone and set up at widely separated sites: at Alexandria, Canopus and Naucratis – the Greek city states in Lower Egypt; at Arsinoë – the City of Crocodiles and the capital of the Greek settlement in the Fayoum; and undoubtedly at Ptolemais (now Minshah) – the Greek city state with a Greek constitution in Upper Egypt.

Towards the end of the Ptolemaic period a change came about. The court, rich in material wealth and lax in morals, became the scene of decadence and anarchy. Meanwhile, across the Mediterranean, Rome was rising as a great power and Egypt began to fall more and more under its influence.

Cleopatra, one of the most colourful characters of the last phase of Ptolemaic rule, was eighteen years old when she came to the throne as a co-regent with her brother Ptolemy XIII. They were under the guardianship of the Roman senate. Filial rivalry led Ptolemy XIII to banish his sister from Egypt. Cleopatra sought refuge in Syria with a view to raising an army and recovering the throne by force of arms. When the ageing Caesar came to Alexandria in 47 BC, he took the part of the banished queen.

It was a short-lived recovery; were it not for the famous love affair between Cleopatra and Mark Antony, Caesar's close friend, the end of the Ptolemaic period might have been obscured. As it was, Antony was declared an enemy of Rome by the Senate and Octavian, Caesar's successor, set sail across the Mediterranean, determined to conquer Egypt once and for all.

Mark Antony had been living in the luxury of the Egyptian court with Cleopatra. He set sail to meet the challenge, but he was no match for Octavian. They met at Actium, on the western coast of Greece, and the battle was fought within sight of the land. Antony was seen to abandon his soldiers, board Cleopatra's royal cedarwood vessel, which was surrounded by its fleet of smaller ships, and make his escape. Rather than face disgrace he commited suicide.

Octavian had no difficulty in capturing Alexandria. Cleopatra, aware that she would be taken prisoner to Rome, is said to have allowed herself to be bitten by a poisonous asp. The Ptolemaic period was over. 'I added Egypt to the dominions of the Roman people' recorded Gaius Julius Caesar Octavianus Augustus, now sole ruler and emperor.

Roman Egypt (30 BC–AD 395)

The Roman occupation of Egypt, while ostensibly a continuation of the Greek, differed markedly from it. While a common recollection of hostility towards the Persians and a long history of commercial relations bound Egyptians and Greeks together, no such affinity existed between Egyptians and Romans. Alexander the Great had come to Egypt without striking a blow. Roman troops had pitched battles with Egyptians almost immediately. The Ptolemaic kings had lived in Egypt; the Roman emperors governed from Rome, and their prefects took over the position formerly held in the scheme of government by the Ptolemaic kings. To the Egyptians, therefore, the prefect and not the emperor, who resided in far-off Rome, was the royal personage.

There was also a drastic change in the climate of leadership. For the Ptolemies had respected the Egyptians and had made friendly gestures, such as bringing back to Egypt some of the sacred objects carried off by the Persians after a military campaign in Asia. The Romans, on the other hand, controlled Egypt by force. They stationed garrisons at Alexandria, which remained capital, Babylon (Old Cairo), which was the key to communications with Lower Egypt; and Syene (Aswan), which, as in the Old Kingdom, became the southern boundary of Egypt.

There was no immediate change in the internal organisation of the country. The Ptolemies had proved that, by reason of its isolated position and internal wealth, Egypt was both a natural and a convenient unit for administration. And the Romans were quick to recognise the benefits of interfering, at first, as little as possible with the existing system. The nomes remained the same and the nomarchs collected the taxes.

However, there slowly evolved a highly complicated structure of sub-divisions into towns and villages, where hordes of officials kept tax records in a system of controls, checks and counter-checks. This was established to fulfill Egypt's required contribution to the Roman treasury every year; the amount was decided by the emperor, and his prefect carried out his orders. The Egyptians had no say in the management of their affairs, and there does not seem to have been any concern for their welfare. Temple lands were annexed and placed under the control of the government. The local priests were allotted only a small part of their sacred property. Their material wealth was curbed by a chief financier – a Roman official acting as high priest who resided in Alexandria.

Meanwhile Alexandria, the one-time peaceful capital and seat of learning, became a turbulent city. Recognising it as a potential trouble area, Roman garrisons were strengthened. The city was deprived of its senate, thus curtailing its political privileges. Egyptian script fell into disuse while Greek was increasingly used.

Egypt maintained the appearance of an Egyptian state, but it was, in fact, no more than a dependancy of Rome. The farmers were pressed to maximum production, wheat shipments to Rome continued, and the prosperity of the country can be traced through the issue of fresh coinage, but still with Greek denominations, originally put into circulation by Augustus (27 BC). But the erosion of the country's resources was critical. Whereas the Ptolemies had based their system of taxation on the productive capacity of the land, with the revenue mostly spent in Egypt, the Roman system of taxation was not based on productivity and was destined to drain the wealth from Egypt for the benefit of Rome.

The Greeks had adopted Egypt as their own country and had kept alive its identity. Under the Romans, an impoverished Egypt was shorn of glory. The Greeks had re-established the crumbling world of the Nile valley as once more the most important country in the eastern Mediterrranean. Under the Romans, Egypt was no more than a granary of the emperor, treated as his private estate, and a pleasure-ground for the Roman upper classes. They visited Egypt in vast numbers. They came to see the Pyramids of Giza, the Apis bull of Memphis, the ancient city of Abydos, the Colossus of Memnon, and the healing centres at Deir el Bahri and Philae.

A keen interest in Egypt and all things Egyptian had developed in Rome long before the conquest. The cults of Isis and Serapis had already made their way across the Mediterranean. All the paraphernalia of their cults were known and had become very popular. Hadrian commissioned a Nilotic landscape for his palace in Tivoli, just outside Rome, and no less than thirteen obelisks were transported to Rome.

While the Romans indulged their passion for revelry, luxury and entertainment, the Egyptians, pressed by the demands of the treasury, were bent to the land unable to meet the increasing taxes. There was undoubtedly a certain hypocrisy in the Egyptian artists who eulogised a Roman emperor with the attributes of the Egyptian pharaoh, when there is no evidence that the emperors were even respected, let alone worshipped as gods in Egypt. There is practically no trace of Roman deities in Egypt, and the few inscriptions of gods, such as Jupiter and Juno, were written as Latin equivalents of Egyptian gods.

It was during the Roman period, especially during the terrible persecutions of Diocletian (AD 284 305), that thousands of Egyptians sought refuge in the deserts and founded the monastic way of life (chapter 8). When the emperor Septimius Severus came to Egypt early in the third century, the complicated control system was in danger of breaking down. Efforts at reorganisation could not turn the tide. The economic situation had so drastically deteriorated by the steady drain on the country's resources that it took extreme reforms to reorganise the government of Egypt.

Constantine the Great (AD 324–337), the first Christian emperor, subdivided Egypt into six provinces under the Bishop of Alexandria. Conditions temporarily improved. Unfortunately, schisms appeared in the Christian church, which led to riot and disorder in Alexandria. The controversy, which was subsequently the main topic of discussion at the Council of Nicaea in AD 325, concerned interpretation of doctrine on the nature of Christ: whether He was begotten by God before all time, and was godlike; or whether Father and Son were of the same nature.

Under the Emperor Theodosius (d. AD 395), Christianity was declared to be the offical religion of Egypt. The Roman empire was transformed and Egypt became a part of the eastern Rome or Byzantine Empire. 'Paganism' was suppressed. Ancient monuments were systematically destroyed, tombs were ravished and walls were plastered to hide the reliefs of the ancient gods.

Augustan birth house at Dendera: Augustus offers a small boat to Isis

Façade of the Temple of Hathor at Dendera

DESCRIPTION

Graeco-Roman Temples in Upper Egypt

Temple of Hathor at Dendera

Dendera (Greek *Tentyra*) is situated on the western bank of the Nile south of Abydos, where the river makes a great curve to the east. Hathor, the sacred cow, was the popular deity.

Evidence of actual temple building at Dendera dates to the Middle Kingdom, and some restoration was carried out in the New Kingdom, when Thutmose III revived the greatly popular ancient 'Voyage of Hathor'. Complete reconstruction, however, was started under the later Ptolemies and was finished some 185 years later under the Roman emperor Tiberius, with the names of other first-century AD emperors appearing on the entrance gateway. It is, therefore, of pure Graeco-Roman style.

The Ptolemies claimed that they were constructing the temple on the site of an ancient monument built by the pharaohs of the Old Kingdom. In fact, in one of the crypts, the name of the 6th Dynasty Pharaoh Pepi I (*c.* 2300 BC) appears. At that time the noblemen of Elephantine were 'Keepers of the Southern Gate', and they recorded collaboration with the local citizens of Dendera, praising them highly.

In dedicating a temple to Hathor, the Ptolemies were honouring one of Egypt's best loved deities. Hathor was sometimes depicted as a cow, sometimes as a female figure with the head of a cow, and later with a woman's head and the ears of a cow. She was a widely popular goddess, and although Dendera was her cult centre, she was well known far afield. In Luxor she was known as 'Lady of the West' and in mortuary scenes is depicted emerging from a mountain range flanking the western desert to welcome the deceased to the underworld. In Memphis her name was 'The Lady of the South Sycamore'; in Punt she was 'Mistress of Punt'; in Sinai 'Mistress of Mefket'; and in Phoenicia she was known as the 'Lady of Byblos'. She was associated with pleasure, motherhood and beauty, often being shown giving suck to a ruling pharaoh or licking his hands (page 75).

As a mother-goddess, Hathor was identified with the Sky-goddess Nut. She was, therefore, also regarded as a cosmic deity. In order to fulfill her dual role of sacred cow and heavenly mother, she was graphically depicted in the tomb of Seti I at Thebes standing over the earth, with her four legs representing the four pillars of the universe; she supports the sun disc on her back and the heavenly bodies on her belly. Hathor was the goddess whose functions and attributes were most often assimilated by other goddesses. She was, in a sense, a national goddess. Her symbol was the sistrum, a rattle, which was probably an ancient musical instrument believed to drive away evil spirits.

The traditions of Hathor of Dendera were closely linked with those of Horus of Edfu (page 171). They were two deities of equal standing, husband and wife. At each site the triad consisted of Hathor, Horus and their son (who bore a different name at each site). At Dendera, however, Hathor was the chief deity, while at Edfu it was Horus. Their son, who was often depicted as a naked child playing with the sistrum, became known as the 'sistrum player'.

Twice a year, on the occasion of the birthday of each deity, the festival of the 'Good Union' was celebrated. This was when the barge bearing the sacred statue of Hathor would be taken out of its shrine at Dendera, placed on a Nile vessel and carried upstream; meanwhile that of Horus would set off downstream, each in a splendid river procession. Where the boats came together, they would be encircled by a rope cast by other vessels, in a gesture of

160

TEMPLE OF HATHOR AT DENDERA Plan 35

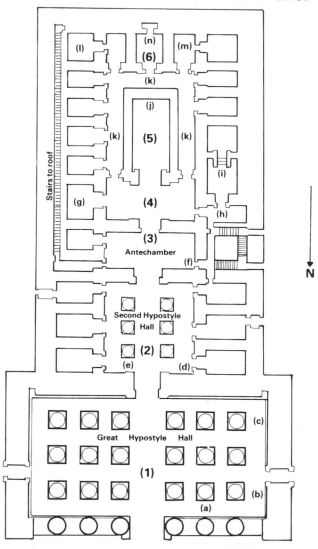

unity. Then, together, the river crafts would make their way to the appropriate temple to celebrate the reunion of husband and wife amidst joy, song and prayer.

The second great festival at Dendera was on 'New Year's Day', when the image of Hathor, which had gradually lost strength in the darkened sanctuary throughout the year, would be taken to the top of the temple to view all her possessions and be reimbued with power from the rising sun.

In the Ptolemaic period Hathor was identified with Aphrodite and began to enjoy immense popularity as 'Mistress of music, dance and joy'. Some of the dignity of Hathor as mother-goddess, sacred to the Egyptians, was lost when her temple became the 'home of intoxication and place of enjoyment'. Among the Roman emperors depicted in the temple are Augustus, Tiberius, Caligula, Claudius and Nero.

The **Temple of Hathor** comprises a Great Hypostyle Hall (1), a second Hypostyle Hall (2), two ante-chambers (3) and (4), leading to a Sanctuary (5), which is enclosed on three sides and surrounded by chambers, some of which may have served as living quarters for priests, others as storerooms for the ritual implements for services.

The entrance to the temple has an impressive façade, on each side of which are three Hathor-columns joined by screen walls. These also form one side of the Great Hypostyle Hall. At the centre of the huge concave cornice is the proclamation that the temple was built by the Emperor Tiberius under his prefect Aulus Avillius Flaccus.

The **Great Hypostyle Hall** (1) has eighteen Hathor columns once painted in brilliant colours; they supported a roof that is divided into seven sections, each of which is decorated with **astronomical scenes**. These are similar to those which adorn most Graeco-Roman temples, but nowhere are they so well preserved as on the ceiling of the Hypostyle Hall at Dendera.

In the *first section* (to the extreme right) is the elongated figure of Nut, the sky-goddess; her body arches over the heavens, and her legs and arms represent the four pillars of the universe. The long line of figures includes six signs of the Egyptian zodiac: the lion, the serpent, the balances, the scorpion, the archer and the goat. There are eighteen ships in the second line in which are the controllers of eighteen sections of ten days; these are the divisions of the half-year. The *second section* has a winged figure representing the wind at each end; here the astronomical figures relate to the twelve hours of night. The controllers are grouped into threes to represent the space of a lunar month. The *third section* concerns the moon, represented as the sacred eye; the fourteen days of the waning moon, followed by fourteen days of the waxing moon, ascending the steps to heaven to approach Osiris, who is seated in a boat with Isis and Nephthys.

The *middle section* of the roof has alternate vultures and discs with wings. The *fifth section* has three rows of figures; among them are twelve boats representing the hours of the day, each bearing the sun disc, and beside each is the deity to which that special hour was sacred. The *sixth section* once again has the winged figure of the wind at each end and astronomical figures between them. The *seventh section*, like the first, shows the elongated figure of Nut, the Sky-goddess, spanning the heavens and, at the northern end, the sun's rays shining on the shrine of Hathor. Among the line of figures represented here are the other six signs of the Egyptian zodiac: the crab, the twins, the bull, the ram, the fishes and the water carrier, and eighteen ships, each bearing *decani*, or controllers of a ten-degree segment of the zodiacal hemisphere, of which there were thirty-six in all.

On the screen walls on the inside of the entrance are reliefs that relate to the ceremonial of 'going forth'. The pharaoh is shown leaving his palace at (a) to visit the temple. He is led by the small figure of a priest who burns incense. In the procession are five tribal standards representing ancient cities: the jackal wolf-god of Thinis (Abydos); the ibis head of Thoth the moon-god of Hermopolis; the hawk of Edfu, the emblem of an ancient goddess of Thebes, and the symbol of the sistrum of Dendera. Horus and Thoth sprinkle the pharaoh with the symbol of Life, and the goddesses of Nekheb and Buto (ancient capitals of Upper and Lower Egypt) bestow their blessings on him.

At (b) the pharaoh is depicted being presented to Hathor by Montu of Thebes and Atum of Heliopolis. He marks out the limits of the temple and drives boundary posts into the ground. The scenes on the right-hand wall (c) show him worshipping the triad at Dendera: Hathor, Horus and their son, here known as Ihy.

The second **Hypostyle Hall** (2) has six columns with richly ornamented, if rather clumsy, capitals. The bases are of granite, the rest of the columns in sandstone. Light is admitted into the hall from eight square apertures in the roof. Some of the reliefs on the walls that relate to the founding of the temple and sacrifices to the gods of Dendera have empty cartouches; the artists did not fill the oblong symbol with the king's name as though uncertain for whom they were carrying out the work, or under whom it would be completed.

The reliefs at (d) should be noted. They show the pharaoh in two representations: one leaving his palace, preceded by the standards representing the ancient cities, and the second showing him breaking ground with a hoe to lay the foundation stone of the temple in the presence of Hathor. On the corresponding wall (e) he is similarly represented but shaping a brick before Hathor. This scene represents a long-standing tradition since shrines built of brick had long given way to temples of stone.

The three small chambers on each side were stores, treasuries or repositories for offerings.

The ante-chamber (3) is decorated with four rows of reliefs of offerings to the deities of Dendera. On both sides there are passages leading to staircases that ascend to the roof of the temple. These were used by the priests during the Festival of the New Year, when, as already mentioned, the statue of Hathor was taken up to the roof in order to gaze upon her possessions and be reimbued with strength from the rising sun.

The tastefully executed reliefs on the walls of the staircases show the procession ascending to and descending from the roof. The pharaoh is led by a priest and followed by others. Some of them wear masks of lesser deities; others spread incense, chant or clap their hands. One priest reads from a papyrus. Behind him a priestess bears two caskets, guarded over by the high priest; he is followed by the second, third and fourth priests in succession.

Then comes the sacred shrine bearing the statue of Hathor. Several priests have the honour of bearing it to the roof of the temple. After the necessary ritual, the procession will descend, and the statue will be returned to the sanctuary.

On the roof an open courtyard leads to two rooms, one of which is the Chamber of Osiris, where there is a graphic portrayal of the death of Osiris, the conception of Horus and the rebirth of the slain leader (see Osiris myth, page 13). The roof of the second chamber has a plaster cast of the famous Zodiac of Dendera set in it. The original was removed by the French and is in the Louvre, Paris.

Retracing our steps to the ante-chamber (3), we pass into ante-chamber (4). The doorway to the left leads to a chamber (g) that contained the garments, perfumes, wreaths and linens used to adorn the statues of the gods, and for use during rituals. To the left, another storeroom (h) leads to a closed sanctuary known as the kiosk. This is a charming structure, supported by two Hathor-columns and approached by seven steps. The walls show the king and various deities in the presence of the gods of Dendera. On the ceiling is a delightful representation of Nut, the Sky-goddess, with

Rear wall of temple, Dendera: Cleopatra and Caesarion

the sun rising from her lap and shining on Hathor's head.

Retracing our steps to the ante-chamber (4), we enter the **Sanctuary** (5) where the sacred boat of Hathor stood. Only the pharaoh himself or the high priest was permitted to enter this holy place, and the scenes to the left and right show how this was done: the king ascends the steps to the shrine, removes the band across the door, breaks the seals, opens the door and, finally, casts his eyes in awe at the sacred statue of the goddess. He prays, offers incense and withdraws.

On the rear wall of the Sanctuary (j), to the left, the son of Hathor plays with his sistrum and with a rattle, and the king offers the image of Maat, goddess of Truth, to Hathor and Horus.

The sanctuary is surrounded by a **corridor** (k). Note the apertures in the side walls and in the ceiling that light it. Eleven storerooms lead off the corridor. The rear central chamber, behind the sanctuary (6), contained a shrine with the image of Hathor; it is decorated with reliefs similar to those of the sanctuary.

The **Crypts** are the subterranean chambers where the treasures of the temple were stored or hidden. There are some dozen in number, and they were constructed with hidden entrances, or approached by narrow flights of stairs. The reliefs are nearly perfect and well worth a visit, although they are difficult of access. (*Visitors would do well to be guided into these places*). They depict the treasures that were stored there: precious statues, symbols of the gods, sacred vessels and jewellery.

Some of the most interesting crypts to the rear of the temple are approached from the Court of the Kiosk (i), from chamber (l) and from chamber (m). The latter leads to the one directly behind the Hathor room (6), and on the right-hand wall is a representation of Pepi, the 6th Dynasty pharaoh, kneeling and offering the golden statuette of the son of Hathor, to four images of Hathor. Such a relief, executed by the Ptolemies, was designed to show that the traditions and rituals being conducted within the temple were of long standing.

The priceless reliefs of some of the crypts, which mostly date to the reign of Ptolemy XIII, were subjected to vicious robbery some twenty years ago. Some reliefs were literally hacked out of the wall, destroying large decorated surrounding areas, and smuggled out of Egypt.

On the outer (south) wall of the temple (n) is the famous relief of Cleopatra (depicted as Hathor) and her son Caesarion (Ptolemy XVI), who was the son of Julius Caesar. There has been much discussion as to whether these figures are accurate portraits or simply conventional representations.

The **Birth House** or **Mammisi** lies to the right, north-east of the main temple. It was constructed by Augustus, with reliefs added by Trajan. The earliest Birth Houses date towards the end of the pharaonic periods and during Graeco-Roman times temples invariably had one.

The reliefs of such buildings relate to the birth of the child Horus, who grew to manhood, overthrew the enemies of his father Osiris and took over the throne of Upper and Lower Egypt. The purpose of stressing this ancient tradition was to show that Horus (who was identified with Egypt's first pharaoh) was the offspring of the gods; consequently, any sovereign who recognised this tradition showed that he, too, should be regarded as a descendant of Horus, and that he ruled by divine sanction. The donning of the necessary crowns and the handing over of sacred insignia by the local priests would indicate their acknowledgement of this right to rule.

The original Birth House at Dendera was built by Nektanebos to the right of the main temple. At the time of the building of the great hypostyle hall, however, it was decided to surround the temple with an enclosure wall; though this was never completed, it nevertheless cut through the tiny Birth House and separated it from the main temple. Another, far more impressive Birth House was forthwith designed to the north. The reliefs of Nektanebos' Birth House, especially those relating to the ram-headed god Khnum modelling the infant king on the potter's wheel, were repeated in the Roman structure.

The Roman Birth House has colonnades with lotus blossoms to the north and south. Between them are finely carved screens showing the emperor offering boats, jewels, et cetera, to Isis, often in the company of Horus the Younger. Bess, patron deity of childbirth, is depicted on the rear wall, flanked by figures of Hathor; this laughing dwarf-like deity was identified with Typhon in Ptolemaic times. He is also depicted standing on the column capitals.

The interior of the Birth House has a vestibule, which leads to an ante-chamber and the rectangular sanctuary where the most interesting scenes are to be found. On the right-hand wall, in the third register, Amon enters, followed by different deities, including Khnum, who leads Hathor by the hand. Thoth summons Hathor, and Amon orders Khnum to fashion the child. As already mentioned (page 37) Khnum, the god of the inundation, became a god of creation in a later tradition, and, on the opposite wall, also in the third register, we can see him modelling the child Ihy (undoubtedly representing the Emperor Augustus). The goddess Sheshat (to the left) writes down the years and (to the right) the child is presented to Hathor.

The Birth House of Augustus was converted into a church in the Christian era; and between it, and the original Birth House of Nektanebos, a Christian Basilica was built. (For ruins of the Christian Basilica at Dendera (see page 209).

Temple of Deir el Medina at Luxor

The area of Luxor, with its powerful priesthood and marvellous monuments on both sides of the Nile, was not the scene of much Graeco-Roman reconstruction. The small, elegant and beautifully preserved temple in the necropolis, known as Deir el Medina, is an exception. It was founded by Ptolemy IV on a site with a long history. It honoured two of Egypt's great sages. These were Amenhotep, son of Hapu, who lived in the reign of Amenhotep III (1390 BC), and Imhotep, builder of the Step Pyramid of Sakkara, wise sage and physician of Zoser's Court well over a thousand years earlier (2686 BC).

Over the doorway from within the First Court is a representation of the rising sun, symbolically depicted as a scarab, being praised by eight sacred apes. The scenes on all the walls depict Ptolemy IV and his wife Arsinoë making offerings to Egyptian deities: Amon-Ra, Hathor and Shu, god of the atmosphere (right-hand wall).

On the screen walls with Hathor-shaped pillars that separate the First from the Second Court, are the two honoured sages, Amenhotep, son of Hapu, and Imhotep.

The three chambers to the rear of the temple are all in painted relief and in a fine state of preservation. The *left-hand chamber* has a particularly noteworthy judgement scene. It shows the soul of the deceased, followed by Maat, walking towards the Court of Justice. A second figure of Maat stands on the threshold in welcome. In the scene of the weighing of the heart of the deceased against the feather of Truth in the scales of justice, Horus and Anubis stand witness. Thoth, the god of wisdom, notes the verdict. Beside the scales are a youthful Horus seated upon the crook that symbolises power, and a fearful monster. In the case of a favourable judgement, it is the young Horus who claims the soul; in the case of failure, the monster has his claim.

Presiding over the trial is, of course, Osiris, god of the underworld. Before him are four genii rising out of a lotus flower.

These are the children of Horus, guardians of the Canopic jars, where the viscera removed during embalming were placed. Above Osiris are the forty-two judges of the dead.

On the opposite, *right-hand* wall, is a representation of a large sacred barge, belonging to Soker-Osiris, resting on a pedestal. In front of it are two standards bearing the emblem of Wepwawat, the ancient god of Abydos, and three other standards behind it. Towards the end of the wall Ptolemy burns incense in an elaborate censer before the figure of the god Min in a shrine. Anubis is clad in a red robe and holds a disc in his hand.

Temple of Khnum at Esna
Esna, the ancient *Seni*, was a centre for local commerce from early times, with open-air market and kiosks. (The Greek *Latopolis*, after the Latus fish that was revered in the area, never came into common usage.)

The importance of Esna dates from 18th Dynasty, when Thutmose III led his army into Nubia, and trade with the south was active. Only in Graeco-Roman times, however, did the area become sufficiently important to justify the building of a temple over some ancient ruins.

This is a small temple, built in honour of Khnum, the Ram-

TEMPLE OF KHNUM AT ESNA Plan 36

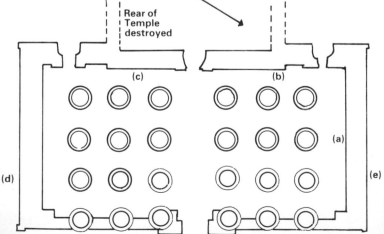

headed god of the cataract region (page 37). Little time is needed to view it. The temple is mainly of historic interest, since the name of the emperor Trajan Decius (AD 249–251) is the last Roman name to appear in a royal cartouche.

The *pronaos*, or first hall, has a decorated roof supported by twenty-four columns in six rows. The first row are joined by balustrades, which form the front wall. The façade faces the Nile. Votive inscriptions for Claudius (AD 41–54) and Vespasian (AD 69–79) appear on each side of the sun-disc on the architrave over the entrance. That of Vespasian refers to him as 'Lord of Rome the Capital'.

The temple lies deep below the present ground level and is approached down a flight of steps. The capitals are elaborate and finely decorated – two feature bunches of grapes. The side walls show Roman emperors, clad in Egyptian dress, performing traditional ceremonies. They lay foundation stones and consecrate the temple. The reliefs, on the whole, are of poor quality. During the Roman period art was fast deteriorating. There was even such careless copying of hieroglyphic inscriptions that some parts of the text defy decipherment. The names of Claudius, Vespasian, Domitian, Trajan, Hadrian, Antoninus Pius, Marcus Aurelius, Commodus, Septimius Severus, Caracalla and Decius all appear. The heavily inscribed columns detail the religious ritual of the temple, preserving much detailed information from earlier times.

On the lower registers of the right-hand wall (a) there is a fine relief that shows the emperor Commodus, depicted as Horus, joining Khnum in drawing in a netfull of waterfowl and fishes. In the net are some of Egypt's enemies that have been caught along with the river creatures. This scene is watched over by Egyptian deities.

The reliefs on the rear wall, which date to Ptolemaic times, are more delicately executed than those of the Roman period. On the *right-hand* wall (b) sacrifices are made to Khnum. On the *left-hand* wall (c) Khnum is being offered a potter's wheel. At the centre of the rear wall is a portal, resembling a pylon, crowned with a concave cornice; the portal originally led to the inner chambers of the temple, which have been destroyed.

On the *outside* side walls of the Temple, to the left and right (d) and (e), the king is shown holding groups of enemies by the hair and smiting them, with lists of the conquered territories below.

(*In the neighbourhood of Esna, Christian hermits lived in the ancient tombs, and several convents and churches were built there*)

Horus on the entrance pylon at Edfu

Temple of Horus at Edfu

Edfu (Greek *Apollonopolis*), which is situated between Esna and Aswan, is a site with a long-standing tradition. Its name is derived from the ancient *Edbo*; it means 'The Town of the Piercing' and refers to the triumph of Horus over Set.

There is evidence of occupation in Edfu from pre-dynastic times through to the end of the Roman period. The temple of Horus, however, is entirely Ptolemaic. Texts on the outer face of the girdle wall indicate that it was begun in 237 BC and completed in 57 BC. Ptolemy III, who started the building, claimed that he was constructing it on an original plan made by Imhotep, builder of Zoser's Step Pyramid at Sakkara that was raised some two thousand five hundred years earlier. The ruins of the ancient town show that the site was, indeed, an important province during the Old Kingdom, and that it retained its importance in the Middle Kingdom.

When the festal journey between Horus of Edfu and Hathor of Dendera was instituted as a regular ceremony in the New Kingdom, Edfu gained great prestige and popularity. This 'Good Reunion' took place in the second month of the Egyptian year, when Hathor of Dendera came to visit her husband Horus in his temple at Edfu. The statue of Horus was placed on the sacred boat that was placed on a Nile vessel to be borne northwards to meet his mate. Hathor's sacred statue was likewise travelling from Dendera towards Edfu. Great was the joy of the populace lining the banks of the river when the craft came together in mid-stream; husband and wife were united.

Amidst joy and celebration the two boats would make their way to Edfu, where the entire population assembled to watch the priests enter the temple with the sacred statues.

The **Temple at Edfu**, along with those of Philae, contains some of the finest art and architecture of the Ptolemaic period. It is dedicated to Horus, Hathor and their son, 'Horus the younger' or 'Uniter of the Two Lands'. It comprises a Great Court (1), the Pronaos (2), Hypostyle Hall (3) and two ante-chambers (4) and (5), leading to the Sanctuary (6). Around the sanctuary is a corridor leading to smaller chambers; around the rear part of the temple runs an Outer Corridor that is accessible only from the Outer Court, or from the two Hypostyle Halls.

The entire temple – corridors, halls, ante-chambers, sanctuary, inner chambers, outer walls – are embellished with wonderful reliefs. This is one of the most beautiful, and certainly the best

TEMPLE OF HORUS AT EDFU Plan 37

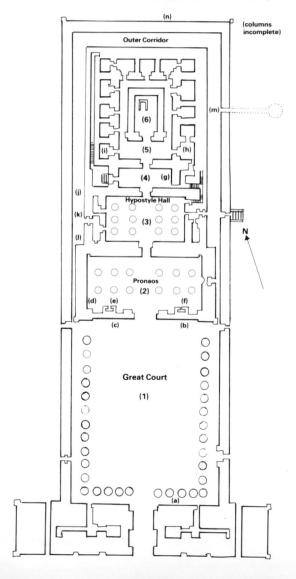

(n)

(columns incomplete)

Outer Corridor

(6)

(m)

(5)

(i)   (h)

(4)   (g)

(j)

Hypostyle Hall

(k)

(3)

N

(l)

Pronaos

(2)

(d)   (e)   (f)

(c)   (b)

Great Court

(1)

(a)

Relief in the outer ambulatory in temple of Horus at Edfu (j)

preserved of Egypt's monuments. In fact there is no ancient monument in the world that can match it.

A large granite statue of Horus the Hawk – one of two found outside the western tower – stands in front of the entrance guarding the temple. On its head is the Double Crown of Upper and Lower Egypt.

The **Entrance Pylon** is completely covered with inscriptions and reliefs, both inside and out. They mostly show Ptolemy XIII in the Egyptian tradition; he clasps enemies by the hair and raises his arm to smite them, in the presence of Horus of Edfu and Hathor of Dendera. (*Access to the top of the pylon can be gained by small stairways approached from outside the temple and from the Great Court, but is not normally accessible.*)

The **Great Court** (1), where offerings were once made to Horus on a great altar, is a spacious enclosure surrounded on three sides by a gallery supported by thirty-two columns. The shafts are decorated with reliefs; the capitals are ornate flower and palm-fronds.

The wall reliefs relate to the Good Reunion between Horus and Hathor; on the lower reaches of the right-hand wall (a) the festal boats of Horus and Hathor may be seen on the Nile; they are towed to Edfu. On arrival, the priests carry the statues, in their barges, towards the temple; there they make offerings and conduct prayers.

To the rear of the Court, Ptolemy IX makes offerings; he presents four libation jars to Horus, and a sphinx to Hathor in the presence of Horus (b). There is a similar scene at (c) with offerings of electrum to Hathor. Before the screen, to the left of the doorway is a superb granite hawk of Horus, distainfully surveying the court.

The central doorway leads to the *Pronaos* (2), the roof of which is supported by columns with various floral capitals, and the ceiling is decorated with astrological scenes. The walls are covered with reliefs that, unfortunately, have lost much of their vivid colour. The themes relate to the consecration of the temple. To the left (d), Ptolemy IX breaks ground with a hoe, before Horus and Hathor. Incense is cast on the broken ground to purify the area. The completed temple is then encircled and blessed, in the presence of Horus.

Two tiny chambers have been built up against the walls to left and right of the entrance. The chamber to the left (e), is the Consecration Chamber. The inscription over the doorway informs us that golden vessels used for purification ceremonies were stored here. These were used when the pharaoh came to participate in the great festivals of Horus, and, in fact, there is a niche in the wall where they were kept. The wall reliefs show the actual purification ceremonies that were performed in the presence of the deities. Afterwards, the pharaoh, crowned King of Upper and Lower Egypt, is shown being led into the Temple of Horus.

The chamber to the right (f), was the library. The inscription over the doorway states that in this chamber the papyrus rolls of Horus and of Harmachis, arranged by the chief ritual-priest for the twelve hours of the day, were stored. From the small size of the niches inside the chamber we can see that the library probably only contained those texts relating to the traditional ceremonies of this particular temple. Over the doorway is a winged sun disc. Immediately beneath are representations (damaged) of the four senses:hearing, sight, taste and reason, each depicted as a human figure honouring the scribe's palette.

Crossing the Pronaos, on the rear doorway we can see representations of Ptolemy IX performing foundation ceremonies before Horus on either side. Above the doorway is a symbolic scene that shows the sun, with the figure of a winged beetle (Kheper), being guided above the horizon by two hawk-headed figures. The gods Thoth, Neith, Wepwawat, Maat and Hathor are shown to the left.

The **Hypostyle Hall** (3) has twelve columns in three rows. They are slender and also have decorative capitals. Note the openings near the top of the walls, and in the ceiling, which admit light to this otherwise darkened place. The scenes on the walls relate to pegging out the limits of the temple by Ptolemy IV, breaking ground and the final presentation to Horus. It would appear that as each Ptolemaic king succeeded to the throne of Egypt, he would repeat these rituals, thus paying honour to the local populace and to their temple. He would then have the scenes depicted on the temple walls. How joyful the people of Edfu must have been when the Ptolemies honoured Horus and brought them prestige.

The New Year Festival is represented on the walls of the two staircases, which are approached from the **first Antechamber** (4). On the walls of the eastern stairway (g) the king, accompanied by priests bearing the standards that represented Egypt's ancient provinces, mounts to the roof. Behind him is a long procession of priests of a lower order, chanting and reciting hymns. Some of them shake sistrums, burn incense or carry offerings.

At the turn of the passage two caskets are being carried; the statues of Horus and Hathor rest on them. Behind and in front of them are priests of a higher order, who burn incense to safeguard the treasures from any evil spirit that might lurk in the temple. The king and queen look anxiously around to ensure that all is well.

Towards the top of the staircase, priests with standards are depicted once again. At the top, the king heads the procession. He will watch the sacred statues being placed on the roof, where they will remain until dawn. The descent from the roof is depicted on the walls of the western stairway, after the statues have been revitalised from the rays of the rising sun.

The **second Antechamber** (5) lies immediately in front of the sanctuary. Turning to the right, six steps lead to a small open court and a tiny chamber (h) which contains superb reliefs of Ptolemy IV and his wife Arsinöe, making offerings to Horus and Hathor. On the right-hand wall they are enthroned. On the left-hand wall they make offerings to the memory of their royal parents: Ptolemy III and Queen Berenice. Over the doorway are seven representations of Hathor beating tamborines. They might be prototypes of the legendary fairy-godmothers.

The chamber to the left (i) is dedicated to Min, the god of fertility, and to Hathor. The scenes relate to the birth of Horus and the mysterious renewing of life.

In the **Sanctuary** (6), the sacred barge of Horus stood on a low altar at the centre. To the left is a magnificent shrine of dark, highly polished granite in which the sacred statue stood. The reliefs on the

176

Reconstruction of the sacred barge of the god Horus, at Edfu

lower reaches of the right-hand wall show the king, Nektanebos II, the last Egyptian pharaoh, who was responsible for building the shrine, as he removes the lock from the shrine, opens the door, stands in reverential attitude before the sacred statue, and makes offerings. The pivot holes to the sides of the door indicate that the chamber once had double doors.

The corridor around the santuary leads to ten small chambers. All are decorated and relate to items placed in them for storage, and their ritual purpose.

The **Outer Corridor** (accessible from (1) and (3)), has reliefs relating to the overcoming of evil – represented by either a crocodile or a hippopotamus – by good, represented by Horus. They may be found to the west of the temple: at (j) Horus is depicted in a boat, and the king on land. Together they spear a hippopotamus which is held on a rope by Isis. At (k) Horus stands on a chained hippopotamus which he spears. At (1) (*where the corridor narrows*) is a relief showing three figures: the first figure kills a hippopotamus with a knife; the second shows the sage Imhotep reading from a sacred text, and the third shows the king fattening a goose for sacrifice. To the east of the temple (m), a staircase leads to an ancient Nilometer.

The **outside of the Temple** is also embellished with reliefs.

GREAT DOUBLE TEMPLE OF SOBEK AND HORUS
Plan 38

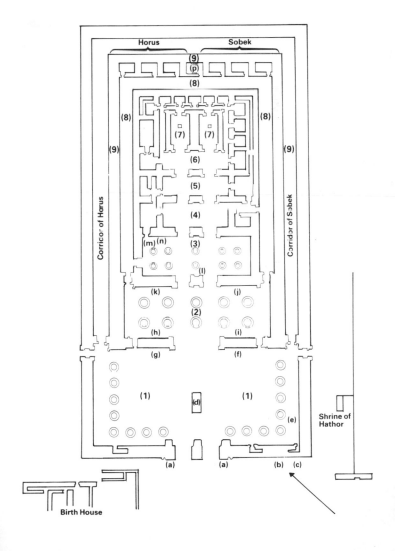

Relief of Horus and Sobek in the Double Temple at Kom Ombo

Those to the rear (n) show Ptolemy XI in the presence of various gods, particularly Horus, Hathor and their son.

Double Temple of Sobek and Horus at Kom Ombo

The ruins of the town of Ombos is situated on a hill that rises some eighteen metres above the surrounding plain **Kom Ombo** (the ancient *Nubyt*) means 'Hill of Ombos'. At this point there is a curve of the Nile with a large island in front of it. This island may once have been a haven for crocodiles that were at first propitiated by the local populace, and then venerated.

Kom Ombo was a site of no great prosperity until Ptolemaic times when it became capital of a separate nome. The town commanded the trade routes in the area and it was, therefore, of strategic importance. The Ptolemies pleased the local populace by building a temple; they had seen much of Egypt's tradition presented in dualistic terms (Double Crown, 'Lord of Two Lands', Upper and Lower Egypt, etc.) and, apparently, saw nothing unusual in building a Double Temple to two hitherto unrelated deities: the hawk god Horwer or Horus the Elder (corrupted to Haroels by the Greeks) and Sobek, the crocodile god. The temple is, in this respect, unique.

The Double Temple is built on a traditional plan but there is an invisible division down the middle; two separate doorways extend its entire length, past the halls and ante-chambers, ultimately leading to two sanctuaries, one to Horus and the other to Sobek. There is evidence that construction and building continued for some four hundred years, the latest Roman emperor featured being Macrinus (AD 217). In addition to the main temple there is a Birth House and a Shrine to Hathor, both of which date to the Roman period.

The **Entrances** face south. The left-hand tower, which is mostly destroyed, depicted scenes relating to the triad headed by Horus the Elder with Isis as his wife and Horus, 'son of Isis', as his son. The right-hand tower shows scenes relating to the triad headed by Sobek with Hathor as his wife, and Khonsu as their son. The triads are depicted on the lower parts of the wall (a). At (b) praises are sung by fifty-two lines of hieroglyphic inscriptions. At (c) a procession is led by the Roman emperor Domitian, as pharaoh. Behind him are Hapi and other deities bearing offerings. In the upper register Domitian leaves the palace, led by a priest who burns incense and is accompanied by priests who bear the tribal standards.

The **Court** (1) is spacious. It has eight columns on each side and an altar near the centre (d). From the vantage of this court one can look northwards through each of the double doors towards the rear of the temple. The eye passes from doorway to doorway, from decorated capital to curved cornice, towards one of the holy sanctuaries. The fine proportions of the temple are best observed this way.

On the right-hand wall (e) is a line of figures of Hapi, led by the pharaoh (in this case Tiberius); each figure bears libation water, bread, cakes and lotus flowers. The screen walls to the rear of the court show the deities pouring libations over Ptolemy XII (Neos Dionysos): on the right-hand wall (f) the deities are the hawk-headed Horus and the ibis-headed Thoth; on the left-hand wall (g) it is Horus (to whom this section of the temple is dedicated) who pays the pharaoh honour. Each section is crowned by a row of uraei, which bear the sun disc on their heads.

The **Great Hypostyle Hall** (2) has ten columns supporting a roof that is decorated with flying vultures along the two main aisles, and astronomical figures beneath the architrave. Attention is drawn to the elegance of the capitals, and their variety of decorative motifs. Many show elaborate palm frond and flower capitals. The wall reliefs are well-preserved; they show all the Ptolemaic rulers who contributed to the decoration of the temple: Ptolemy VI (Philo-

A relief from the Double Temple at Kom Ombo

meter), Ptolemy IX (Euergetes II) and Ptolemy XII (Neos Dionysos).

The reliefs on the inside of the temple, which date to Ptolemaic times, are finer than the crude sunken reliefs on the outer walls of the temple, which date to Roman times. The best reliefs of the Ptolemaic period may be seen at (h). Ptolemy XII stands in the presence of Horus; he receives the symbol of Life from Isis (depicted in the form of a cat) and Nut, the Sky-goddess. The goddesses place their arms around the pharaoh. Thoth and Horus, 'son of Isis', stand behind them.

The corresponding scene (at i) is less carefully worked and not as well preserved. It shows the king being crowned by two ancient goddesses: the vulture-goddess of the pre-dynastic capital of Upper Egypt, and the serpent-goddess of the pre-dynastic capital of Lower Egypt.

To the rear (j) and (k) are scenes of sacrifices and offerings; those to the right relate to the triad headed by Sobek, and those to the left, to the triad headed by Horus.

Unfortunately the two sanctuaries (7) are in a poor state of preservation. Horus's granite pedestal stood to the east, and Sobek's to the west. Between the two sanctuaries, a hidden corridor has been built into the thickness of the wall. This secret place could only be approached from a chamber situated immediately to the rear, where a portion of the floor could be raised to admit a priest to a passage below ground level. The priest must have played a part in the oracular power attributed to the two deities.

The inner corridor (8) leads to seven chambers to the rear of the temple; access is gained from (2) and (3). The entire corridor is decorated with reliefs, some unfinished. (The central chamber (p) has a stairway leading to the upper level.)

The outer corridor (9) is also decorated throughout. It is approached from the Court (1). Here again, the scenes on the left-hand corridor relate to Horus and those to the right to Sobek.

182

The finely decorated capital of one of the columns of the colonade

CHAPTER 7 PHILAE

BACKGROUND

The tiny island of Philae, a mere 450 metres long and less than 150 metres wide, captured the imagination of countless travellers to Egypt from early times. It was famed for its beauty and was known as the 'Pearl of Egypt'. Plants and palm trees grew from the fertile deposits that had collected in the crevices of the granite bedrock. Gracious Graeco-Roman temples and colonnades, kiosks and sanctuaries rose proudly against the skyline. There was a sense of mystery. Not furtive, inviolate secrets, so much as veiled mystification.

The sanctity of Philae during the Graeco-Roman period out-rivalled many of the other cities of Egypt. It had become the centre of the cult of Isis, which was revived during the Saite period (664–525 BC). The Ptolemies, as already noted, sought to please the Egyptians by building temples to their most beloved gods and goddesses.

Ptolemy II (285–246 BC) started construction of the main Temple of Isis. A temple to her consort, Osiris, was built on a neighbouring island, Bigeh (only a portal of which remains). Their son Horus, or Harendotus as he was called by the Ptolemies, had a temple of his own on Philae. Other structures on the island included a small temple to Imhotep, builder of Zoser's Step Pyramid at Sakkara, who was later deified as a god of medicine, and temples to two Nubian deities: Mandolis and Arhesnofer.

Philae was situated south of Aswan and, therefore, strictly belonged to Nubia. Isis was worshipped by Egyptians and Nubians alike. Fantastic tales were told of her magical powers. It was believed that her knowledge of secret formulae had brought life back to her husband Osiris; that her spells had saved her son Horus from the bite of a poisonous snake; and that she was the protectress of all who sought her.

Countless visitors came to the island, where the priests, appropriately clad in white vestments, claimed a knowledge of the mysteries. With carefully rehearsed liturgies and the necessary symbolism, they drew hordes of faithful. If these visitors were lucky they could view the image of the goddess during the spring and autumn festivals in her honour. This was when the death and resurrection of Osiris was enacted, in which Isis played a major role. It was Isis who found the body of her husband that had been locked in a chest and cast on the Nile by his wicked brother Set. It was she who made the body whole through her prayers. It was she who knew the secrets, the spells, and even the name of the Sun-god. Isis was the great goddess; she was at once mother-goddess and magician. It was believed that her single tear, shed for Osiris, caused the annual flood, which brought life to the land.

The myth of Osiris and Isis had, by this time been enlarged and embellished countless times. In one version the coffin containing the body of Osiris was swept out to sea, and came to rest on the Phoenician coast where a tamarisk tree enclosed the entire coffin in its trunk. The king of Byblos, who needed a strong prop for the roof of his palace, ordered the tree to be cut down. Were it not for the fact that the tree gave off a sweet-smelling odour, which spread across the Mediterranean, and reached Isis, she would never have been able to trace the body of her husband. She set off for Byblos without delay and, disguised as a nurse, she took charge of the newborn son of the king. When she finally revealed who she was, and the reason for her being there, the king gave her the miraculous tree containing the coffin, and she took the body of Osiris back to Egypt. This was when Set found it, and cut it to pieces.

Once established on the island of Philae, the priests lost no time in laying claim to additional territory: over eighty kilometres lying to the south of Seheil island. They found an ancient tradition on which to base their claim. In a forged inscription inscribed high on the rocks of Seheil, is a record of how a governor of Elephantine appealed to the pharaoh Zoser (builder of the Step Pyramid some 2,500 years earlier) because of his concern for the people following years of famine. Zoser responded by enquiring about the sources of the Nile and asked whether the governor knew which god controlled its waters. The governor promptly responded that it was Khnum of Elephantine but that he was angry because his temple had been allowed to fall to ruin. Zoser forthwith issued a decree granting a large tract of land to Khnum and levying a tax on all those who lived on the produce of the river, fishermen and fowlers alike, for the benefit of the priests of Khnum. It was this land that the priests of

Philae claimed had been granted *to them* by the pharaoh Zoser, and for the same reason: to put an end to the famine that had been raging for seven long years. The taxes on fishermen forthwith went to their benefit.

Each day the priests would wend their solemn way into the holy precincts of the temple of Isis with incense and burnt offerings. The statue of the goddess would be ceremoniously washed, clothed and adorned. Service after service, ritual after ritual, with humility, chanting and prayer, she would be suitably appealed to and adored until such time as she was undressed, washed again, derobed and replaced in the sanctuary until the following morning.

Little wonder that with such pageantry, with priests shuffling between columns, pouring libations on sacred altars, and swearing to direct communication with the gods, the site should attract curious visitors along with the faithful. Sightseers came in such number as to disturb the priests of Philae. On the base of two granite obelisks found on the island are inscriptions addressed to Ptolemy IX (171–163 BC), his wife and sister, both of whom were called Cleopatra; they complained that:

'. . . . *travellers who visit Philae, generals and inspectors . . . chief officers of the police . . . the armed guards who are following, and the rest of their servants, compel us to pay the expenses of their maintenance while they are here, and by reason of this practice the temple is becoming very poor and we are in danger of coming to possess nothing . . . We beseech you . . . that you give command not to annoy us with these vexations . . . to give us a written decision'.*

A second inscription shows that their wishes were granted, and a third indicates satisfaction at the arrangements made to safeguard them from annoyance.

These Greek and hieroglyphic inscriptions on the base of the obelisks played a part in the decipherment of hieroglyphics. The Rosetta Stone alone was not the key, despite its three copies of a single text in hieroglyphics, demotic and Greek that led to the identification of the word 'Ptolemy'. William Bankes, an English traveller, scholar and collector, to whose estate the obelisk was taken (having been retrieved by Giovanni Belzoni), sent copies of the Greek and Egyptian texts to different scholars, pointing out the hieroglyphic form of 'Cleopatra'. These two names, and others, eventually made it possible to identify seventeen of the twenty-five letters of the hieroglyphic alphabet. The obelisk now stands in the park of Bankes's house at Kingston Lacy in Dorset, England.

*(Habachi, L. 'The Obelisks of Egypt' Scribner 1977; Dent 1978)

Building operations on Philae continued throughout the Roman period. There seems to have been an effort to indicate both continuity of rule, and also to retain the support of the powerful priests on the island near the southern frontier. It was at this time that Plutarch, the Greek writer, came to Egypt, and combined the many variations of the Osiris myth, from the earliest version (page 13) to the later (page 184), into a coherent tale. By this time Osiris had become the just and wise ruler, not of Egypt alone, but of the whole world. He left Egypt under the wise council of Isis, and, accompanied by Thoth, Anubis and Wepwawat, he set off to conquer Asia. He returned to Egypt only after he had spread civilization, peacefully, with song and music, far afield. It has been suggested that this aspect of the myth so closely resembles the stories of Dionysus and Orpheus that Plutarch may have been influenced by them.

The access to the island was enlarged on its northern side by Diocletian, in whose reign the Christians were persecuted. It is ironical that this uniquely picturesque sanctuary was the only peaceful spot in an area that had known nothing but strife from the Persian period (525 BC) onwards. The Meroitic Kingdom had spread northwards and challenged Egypt (page 130). Desert tribes, known as the Blemmys and the Nobadai, who habitually warred with one another, made their appearance around Aswan and terrorised Upper Egypt. There was no security along the frontier.

It is not surprising, therefore, that the island of Philae, isolated and protected from attack and showing a spirit of tolerance to the worship of various gods, should develop a conciliatory character. It was chosen as the venue for the signing of peace treaties; Augustus, the first Roman emperor of all Egypt, ordered his prefect to come to terms with representatives of the Meroitic Kingdom, and the meeting took place on Philae; later, negotiations were conducted there between Roman officials and the Blemmys. It is noteworthy, however, that even in times of conflict, the priests of the Blemmys were given right of entry to the island, and they came in peace.

Garrisons and treaties notwithstanding, the attacks of the Blemmys were renewed year after year. Finally, Diocletian considered it a waste of manpower to keep soldiers stationed in a non-revenue raising area. He ordered their withdrawal. But not before inviting the Nobadai, the long-standing enemies of the Blemmys, to settle in the area and act as a buffer. The Nobadai were provided with a subsidy for their services and the fortifications were strengthened.

As so often happens, a common enemy breeds understanding. The Nobadai and the Blemmys reasoned that nurturing hostility towards one another was getting them nowhere. If they united their forces and attacked Roman Egypt, they might benefit. This they did. Only when Christianity officially came to Egypt under Theodosius (AD 379–395) (page 202), were the two tribes driven out. The Blemmys, however, obtained permission to visit the temple of Isis for certain festivities and, once a year, to borrow the sacred statue of the goddess to consult the oracle.

From a Greek inscription in the seclusion of the Osiris shrine above the sanctuary of the temple of Isis, we learn that in AD 453 the goddess Isis was still worshipped by the Blemmys and their priests. This was long after the edict of Theodosius declared that pagan temples should be closed.

Thus, just as Abydos stands at the beginning of pharaonic history, having given rise to the Thinite kings who first united the Two Lands into a single state, Philae stands at the end, as the last outpost of ancient Egyptian tradition on its native soil.

In the reign of Justinian (AD 527–565) Narsus finally closed the temple and transported statues of some of the deities to Constantinople.

Saving the monuments of Philae

The first Aswan Dam (*El Khazan*) was built between 1898–1902. This was when Philae was first threatened. Poets and writers lamented its destiny but their words fell on deaf ears. Between 1907–1912 the dam was heightened, and fears for the remains of all Nubia were voiced. The Egyptian Government set aside funds to survey, record and, whenever possible, excavate the endangered areas. At this time Philae was inundated for part of each year, from December to August. When it did emerge from the waters of the Nile, it appeared sorrowfully shorn of its vegetation. The picturesque ruins rose from black silt-laden soil with not a shrub nor tendril to break their barren appearance.

Between 1929–34 the Aswan Dam was raised another ten metres, to a height of 44.5 metres. Philae was now inundated for most of the year. Only the high pylon of the temple of Isis, and the kiosk of Trajan, situated at its highest point, could be seen. Small boats could, with difficulty, sail beneath the great architraves. The capitals of the lofty columns alone hinted at what architectural treasures lay beneath the water. Being constructed of sandstone, submersion caused no lasting damage. In fact, the monuments strengthened from contact with water. And the silt which packed against the reliefs, though stripping them of colour, actually protected them.

The decision to build the High Dam (*Saad El Aali*) in 1960 (page 47) caused attention to be focused once again on the fate of Philae. For now, with the constant high level of the water, the monuments would be totally inaccessible. Moreover, the swirling currents from the High Dam that was built south of the island and the existing Aswan Dam to the north would cause them irreparable harm, if not bring about their total collapse.

Egypt launched an international appeal through UNESCO. Philae was brought into the limelight. Projects for saving the monuments were many and varied. All were studied. One project was to build a protective dam on the west, cutting off the island from the main flow of the river and, theoretically, letting it rest in a lower-level lake of its own. This project was abandoned on the grounds that constant pumping out of water would be required to keep the lake at a constant level. The final decision was to dismantle the monuments and re-erect them on another island: Agilkai, slightly to the north of Philae.

An Italian contracting company was chosen to carry out the work. They started with the construction of a coffer dam in 1977. The water was then pumped out, and when the greyish-green blocks were exposed they were dissected, stone by precious stone (forty-seven thousand in number), cleaned, treated, marked and stored.

During the dismantling operations, many blocks of earlier monuments were found to have been reused, especially in the foundations of the buildings. For example, a kiosk dating from the 26th Dynasty during the reign of the pharaoh Psamtik II (594–588 BC) was found dismantled and reused on the western part of the island. Beneath the flagstones of the hypostyle hall of the temple of Isis, another temple, also dating from the 26th Dynasty, was brought to light. Nektanebos, the first ruler of the last, 30th Dynasty (387–361 BC) had reused granite and sandstone blocks inscribed with the names of Amenhotep II, III and Thutmose III for his own constructions on the island, but these had come from temples elsewhere since Herodotus made no mention of Philae when he visited Aswan in the mid-fifth century BC.

While dismantling operations continued, the Egyptian High Dam Company blasted 450,000 cubic metres of granite off the top of Agilkai island. They used some of this to enlarge part of the island to resemble the shape of Philae in order to contain the monuments without distortion. The stones from the dismembered temples were

Reconstructed monuments of Philae

then transported to their new home, and, in a record of thirty months, have been re-erected in an even more perfect condition than before, for many of the reused or fallen blocks that were located were used to reconstruct the original temples.

In March 1980, following an impressive public inaugural ceremony, Philae was declared open to the public. Visitors may once again view the elegant colonnades, the celebrated kiosk and the magnificent Temple of Isis. Soon, when plants take root, the 'Pearl' will once again fit the description of Amelia Edwards who wrote in 1873/74:

'*Seen from the level of a small boat, the island, with its palms, its colonnades, its pylons, seems to rise out of the river like a mirage. Piled rocks frame it on either side, and purple mountains close up the distance. As the boat glides nearer between glistening boulders, those sculptured towers rise higher and ever higher against the sky. They show no sign of ruin or of age. All looks solid, stately, perfect.*'*

DESCRIPTION OF MONUMENTS

The monuments of Philae cover four major epochs: the last part of the Pharaonic era, the Ptolemaic period, the Roman epoch and the

*(A Thousand Miles up the Nile — 2nd ed. N.Y. p. 207)

CHIEF MONUMENTS ON THE ISLAND OF PHILAE
Plan 39

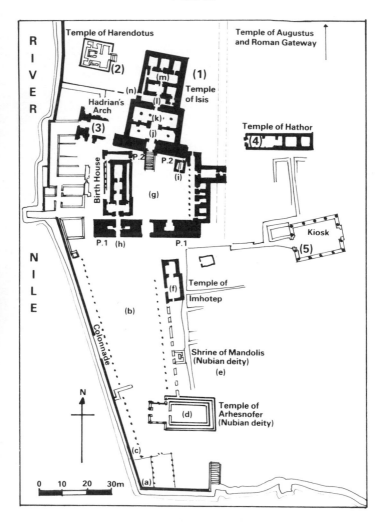

Christian period. The chief monuments are the Temple of Isis (1) and her son Horus (Harendotus) (2), the beautiful Arch of Hadrian (3), the Temple of Hathor (4) and the Kiosk (5), which is also known as Pharaoh's Bed.

The **Entrance** to the island (a) was originally constructed by Nektanebos, the first ruler of the last Dynasty; it was designed with fourteen columns and two sandstone obelisks on the river front. Unfortunately, a particularly high flood swept the structure away soon after it was completed, and it lay in ruin until Ptolemy II had it restored; some of the columns were reconstructed. These have double capitals; the lower parts are decorated with different floral forms and the upper bear heads of Hathor. The screen walls between the columns, crowned with concave cornices bearing rows of uraeus serpents, show Nektanebos making offerings to the deities.

We now stand on the threshold of Philae. Before us a great **Outer Court** (b) opens up. This leads to the Temple of Isis about one hundred metres ahead. The court is flanked by colonnades. On the *right* only half a dozen of the planned sixteen columns were completed; also to the right are the temples of Arhesnofer (d), Mandolis (e) and Imhotep (f).

To the *left*, the thirty-two columns of the colonnade follow the shore line. No two capitals are alike. The shafts show Tiberius making offerings to the Egyptian gods. The ceiling is decorated with stars and flying vultures. The representations are all finely executed and mostly well preserved. For example, between the first two columns (c), above the window, Nero is depicted offering two eyes to Horus, Isis and 'The Lord of the Two Lands'.

The Isis Temple Complex

The huge **Entrance Pylon** (P. 1) lies ahead. It is eighteen metres high and forty-five metres wide. Each of the two towers is decorated with mighty figures of Neos Dionysos, Ptolemy XII, depicted as pharaoh and wearing the Double Crown of Upper and Lower Egypt. He clasps enemies by the hair and raises his club above their heads to smite them in the presence of Egypt's best loved deities: Isis and Nephthys, Horus and Hathor. Thus did the Ptolemaic kings give themselves credit for suppressing Egypt's traditional enemies and honouring local traditions.

Two granite lions guard the entrance; they are of late Roman times and reflect Byzantine influence. On the lintel of the gateway between the two towers of the pylon is a representation of the pharaoh Nektanebos I in a dancing attitude in front of Osiris, Isis,

Khnum and Hathor. Much of the dignity and austerity of the divine pharaoh as the powerful and unapproachable 'Son of the Sun-god', was lost during the Late Period, when representations tended to show informal attitudes.

Passing through the gateway, we come to the **Great Court** (g). To the right is a colonnade and priests' quarters. To the left is the Birth House (which may also be approached from a doorway at the centre of the left-hand tower of the entrance pylon (h).

The **Birth House** is an elegant little building. The entrance portico has a roof supported by four columns and is followed by three chambers, one behind the other. Around three sides of the building runs a colonnade with floral capitals surmounted with sistrum capitals and Hathor heads. The reliefs throughout the building relate to the birth of Horus, son of Isis, and his growth to manhood to avenge his father's death. All are in a fine state of preservation.

The first chamber is not decorated. In the second some quaint protective deities are depicted among the papyrus plants where Horus was born. In the third chamber is a scene (on the rear wall near the bottom) showing Isis giving birth to her son in the marshes of the Delta. With her are Amon-Ra and Thoth. Behind Amon-Ra is the serpent goddess of Lower Egypt and the god of 'wisdom'. Behind Thoth is the vulture goddess of Upper Egypt and the god of 'reason'. Above this scene Horus, as a hawk, stands among the papyrus plants crowned with the Double Crown.

On the *left-hand* wall the standing child Horus suckles at the breast of Isis. Ptolemy IX (Euergetes II) hands two mirrors to Hathor, who places her hands in blessing on the head of the child.

The colonnade surrounding the Birth House is completely decorated. The scene at the beginning of the right-hand colonnade shows the youthful Horus, nude, but wearing the Double Crown. He is with his mother Isis before the serpent goddess of Buto, who plays the harp to them. Augustus stands behind the serpent goddess carrying a vase. The relief of a cow in the marshes that is depicted above the vase indicates the ornamentation within it.

Returning to the Great Court (g) we approach the **Second Pylon** (P. 2) which is smaller in size than the entrance pylon and is not aligned with it. To the right (i) is a large granite block inscribed by the Kushite pharaoh Taharka (730 BC), which is therefore the earliest piece of work on the island. Constructed into the base of the right-hand tower, is a large rock. It is inscribed with the text about the tithe on fishermen. Beyond lies the Isis temple proper.

The god Bess was popular in Graeco–Roman times. (Court of the Temple of Isis)

The Temple of Isis comprises a tiny open court (j), a hypostyle hall (k), an ante-chamber (l) and a sanctuary (m). The walls have fine reliefs of the Ptolemaic kings and Roman emperors repeating traditional, and by now familiar – if not somewhat wearisome — ritual scenes relating to offerings to the Egyptian gods, staking out the temple and consecrating the sacred area.

The Hypostyle Hall (k), which is separated from the court by screen walls between the first row of columns, is adorned with coloured relief from the lower to the upper reaches of the wall, across the ceiling, and from shaft to capital. The columns and capitals provide a good example of the style, decoration and colouring of the Graeco-Roman period, when less regard was paid to natural colours. For example, the blue ribs of the palms stand out somewhat garishly from the light-green palm twigs on the capitals of the columns.

This hall was converted into a church in the Christian Period, when the wall reliefs were covered with stucco and painted. Christian crosses were chiselled in the walls and on some of the columns. In fact, a Greek inscription on the right-hand side of the doorway leading to the ante-chamber (l) records the 'good work' (of destruction of pagan reliefs!) carried out by the Bishop Theodorus in the reign of Justinian, in the fifth century AD.

The sanctuary (m) has two tiny windows and a pedestal on which the sacred barge bearing the statue of Isis stood. This pedestal was installed by Ptolemy III (Euergetes I) and his wife Berenice. Surrounding the sanctuary are the usual priestly chambers and storerooms.

Above the sanctuary are the **Osiris Chambers**, which are approached from a stairway to the left of the temple (n) but currently closed to visitors. In these chambers interesting reliefs relate to the death of Osiris and his rebirth. Among the scenes are: Osiris among the reeds where his body came to rest; the body lying on a bier being prayed over by the jackal-headed Anubis along with Isis and her sister Nephthys; Isis and Nephthys spreading their wings beside the bier as Osiris regains his powers. It is to such graphic portrayals of ancient Egyptian traditions by the Ptolemies that we owe much of our interpretation of ancient Egyptian mythology.

To the left of the stairway (n) is a doorway leading out of the Temple of Isis. A road leads to the temple of Horus (Harendotus), son of Isis (2), and **Hadrian's Gateway** (3). The latter contains the famous relief relating to the source of the Nile on the right-hand wall, in the second row from the top. It shows blocks of stone heaped one upon the other, and standing on the top is a vulture (representing Upper Egypt) and a hawk (representing Lower Egypt), beneath the rocks is a circular chamber which is outlined by the contours of a serpent, within which Hapi, the Nile-god, crouches. He clasps a vessel in each hand, ready, at the appointed time, to pour the water from the 'eternal ocean' to earth in his urns.

The Temple of Hathor
To the right of the temple of Isis, is a large, circular castor-oil presser. The oil was used for medicinal purposes. The **Temple of Hathor** (4) has lively and charming representations, as befitted the goddess of love and joy. The columns are decorated with flute-players and with representations of the laughing dwarf-deity Bes, playing a tambourine and a harp. Apes play the lyre, priests carry an antelope, and Bes dances.

Elsewhere in Egypt, the early Christians were escaping from Roman persecution (page 201). They were abandoning their worldly possessions and fleeing to the desert. But here, on the island of Philae, a spirit of light-hearted joy prevailed.

The famed Kiosk of Trajan

The Kiosk (Pharaoh's Bed)

The Kiosk of Trajan (5) is rectangular in shape and surrounded by fourteen columns with floral capitals. These support blocks that carry the architraves and cornice. The blocks were undoubtedly planned to be carved into sistrum capitals, but they were left unfinished, as were other parts of the structure. The emperor Trajan (AD 98–117) is depicted burning incense in front of Osiris and Isis and offering wine to Isis and Horus.

This is possibly the most graceful of the many elegant buildings on the island, and the one for which Philae is most remembered.

MEDIAEVAL TRADITION

Christianity finally came to the island of Philae and, after the Arab conquest, many of its inhabitants embraced Islam. There being no further need for isolation from the mainland, the population gradually dwindled. By the Middle Ages the island was deserted. It was then that there developed a tale that is strongly reminiscent of the myth of Isis, searching for her loved one Osiris.

It was said that a certain Zahr el-Ward, 'Rose Blossom', beautiful daughter of a grand vizier, fell in love with a young man called Anas el-Wogud. The youth was not accepted by the girl's father who, to protect his daughter, shut her up in the temple of Isis on Philae and told her lover she had gone away.

Anas was not content with the explanation and searched the country for her. Through the Delta and Upper Egypt he went, searching everywhere, until he finally found her on the island. Unfortunately he could not cross the river which was filled with crocodiles, and it was only because he was known throughout the land for his kind and tender heart, and his love of all creatures, that one of the crocodiles allowed him to climb on its back and swim across the river with him.

Meanwhile the beautiful Zahr el-Ward had been planning her escape. Not knowing that her lover knew her whereabouts, she managed to slip out of the temple and find a boat. It is fortunate that the crocodile bearing the lover and the boat bearing the girl met in midstream, where they were reunited much as Horus and Hathor were annually reunited in the 'Good Union' (pages 159, 171).

When the father realised that he could not come between the lovers, he allowed the wedding to take place in the Osiris Room on the roof of the sanctuary of the temple of Isis.

PART III

CHAPTER 8   CHRISTIAN PERIOD

BACKGROUND

Upper Egypt is studded with monasteries, hermitages and churches, some of which date to the 4th and 5th centuries. As a
descriptive guide to the antiquities of Upper Egypt, this book would
therefore fall short of its purpose if it did not cover, however
selectively, some of the early Christian monuments that lie within
easy access of the sites described, and identify some of the pharaonic
temples that were converted into churches.

The historical background given below is by no means a
comprehensive summary of the development of Christianity in
Egypt, which, according to tradition, was introduced by St Mark in
the reign of Nero (AD 54–68); nor does it enter into the theological
disputes that ultimately led to the separation of the Egyptian
Christians (Orthodox Copts) from the Eastern Church of the
Roman Empire. Its purpose is to trace the cultural continuum; to
show why the Egyptians under Roman occupation were so ready to
embrace a doctrine that offered hope; to indicate some details of
iconography – the art of religious illustration – that were drawn
from indigenous sources; and to identify certain architectural
features which reflect inspiration from earlier times.

Egypt under the Romans

In the first century AD, Egypt was under Roman domination.
Alexandria, the harbour capital, had acquired a new source of
wealth as a commercial station between India, Arabia and Rome.
But an immense burden was placed on the Egyptian people in the
form of taxes. The most pressing of these was the wheat tax that was
collected directly from the farmer as part of the quota for Rome.

The produce of the vineyards, palm groves and fig plantations were also collected by Roman officials. Taxes were levied on domestic animals – sheep, oxen, horses and donkeys. Traders were taxed. Oil-sellers, bakers, spice and perfume sellers were taxed. Even the land for garden produce was taxed.

Hunting and fishing licences swelled the resources of the Roman state, and the Egyptians had to pay for the right even to go fowling in the marshes or fishing on the lake – activities their ancestors had enjoyed for thousands of years.

The Upper Egyptians never accepted submission to Roman rule lightly. As early as 29 BC, in the reign of Augustus, there was an insurrection in Thebes against tax collectors. The repercussions were drastic. Within five days, five neighbouring towns were totally razed. Little wonder that so many Egyptians found it more expedient to court the new rulers, and to give orders for their artists to depict them on temple walls in the manner of the ancient pharaohs, honouring the gods and defeating traditional enemies.

Egypt had no leadership in the sense of a recognised pharaoh who preserved order. The people reaped but gained no reward. They were obliged to hand over their grain to Roman troops stationed on

Lintel above a doorway in the Coptic church at Dendera

their soil. They wove fabrics for Roman tunics. Animal hides went for Roman armour. Temple lands were confiscated and then leased out to the farmers.

Many Nile valley dwellers sought refuge in the desert. Some took up life in caves and ancient tombs which, from ancient times had provided convenient habitation, and, from the Ptolemaic period had been used by groups of people seeking isolation. The climatic conditions, especially in Upper Egypt, made it possible to live outdoors, and the wide stretches of quiet desert provided an ideal atmosphere for escape and meditation.

The Gnostics and the discovery at Nag Hammadi

The development of Christianity in Alexandria is cloaked in obscurity; its diffusion throughout the Nile valley is even more so. Christian thought, however, was greatly influenced by the scholarly environment of Alexandria. The first unified translation of the Old Testament into Greek was made there around 250 BC, in the reign of Ptolemy II (when Manetho compiled The Table of Kings (page 8)), and it was in Alexandria that the first and earliest attempt was made to provide a rational basis for faith: to explain the mysteries of revealed truth in the light of intellectual scrutiny. In other words, to explain Christianity in intellectual and philosophic terms.

The Gnostics (from the Greek 'knowledge'), both Christian and non-Christian, drew on a broad spectrum of heritages. They embraced Greek philosophical concepts, pagan literature and mystery cults of the Graeco-Roman world, local Egyptian scripts and folklore, and the Old and New Testaments. They were branded as heretics in the second century, and when the Romans, in the name of orthodoxy, later destroyed the Gnostic settlements – which had by that time spread to Upper Egypt – they destroyed as much of their literature as they could find. As a result, a great gap was left in our knowledge of the early development of Christianity, especially the first two centuries. It is fortunate, therefore, that some of their literature has survived and has been recovered in recent years.

A remarkable discovery was made in 1947. According to one account a huge boulder had fallen onto the slope of the Gebel el-Tarif, a range of hills east of Nag Hammadi, and beneath it peasant farmers found a jar. Inside were codices, or books, that have become known as the Nag Hammadi Library (now conserved in the Coptic Museum in Cairo). The texts, originally written in Greek and later translated into the Egyptian language, were written on papyrus scrolls that were cut into sheets, folded and then bound in leather.

NAG HAMMADI AND ENVIRONS Plan 40

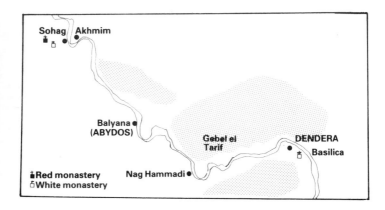

Sohag / Akhmim

Balyana ●
(ABYDOS)

Gebel el
Tarif

DENDERA
● ☥ Basilica

♯ Red monastery   Nag Hammadi ●
♭ White monastery

There are twelve books, each containing collections of essays that vary widely and present divergent viewpoints. They range from a 'secret book' of St John, to the Gospel of Thomas. The former seeks to explain the presence of evil in the world. It describes a cosmology in which there are endless emanations from the ultimate power, which is beyond comprehension and can only be explained by a series of negations. The universe, however, was created, not by this unapproachable, ultimate power, but by a misguided, malevolent and ignorant god.

The Gospel of Thomas is a compilation of sayings attributed to Jesus. In the opening passage is the claim that the words were spoken by the Living (post-resurrection) Jesus to Thomas Didymus Judas, who wrote them down.

The discovery at Nag Hammadi will undoubtedly accelerate the interpretation of early Christianity especially when it is studied in relation to another recent discovery of relevant texts, the Dead Sea Scrolls. More important, the texts will show the Gnostic vision as presented, not by orthodox Christianity, but by the Gnostics themselves.

The difference between the Gnostics and the Christians may be explained as follows: the Gnostics saw a contaminated world that they regarded as the creation of an evil power. They sought spiritual clarity in an esoteric experience. The Christians, on the other hand, saw the same evil world and offered to the despairing people hope of a personal salvation and its promised rewards in the next world. Gnosticism was a religion of escape for an élite minority. Christianity was a religion of hope.

St Paul
The first of the great persecutions started in the reign of Trajan Decius (249–251). The number of Egyptians who escaped to the deserts increased. Among them was St Paul, the Theban, a native Egyptian who spoke Greek only with the greatest difficulty (as distinct from the Hellenized Egyptians in Alexandria). He chose a remote site on the Red Sea coast, where he founded a hermitage. By this time thousands of 'anchorites' (derived from the Greek root 'retire' or 'withdraw') were either living alone or in small groups, isolated from one another. Slowly individual ascetics started to draw near to one another to look for guidance from a master, and St Paul gave instruction in an atmosphere of security and spirituality. After St Paul came St Anthony, who also chose a site near the Red Sea rather than the Nile valley. His famous biography was written by his friend Athanasius, eloquent deacon of the Bishop of Alexandria (AD 325) and his life and teachings strongly influenced those of the desert fathers.

During the brutal persecutions of Diocletian, who reigned from 284 to 305, many chose martydom rather than make offerings to the hated emperors. There is little doubt that Christianity flourished on the willingness to suffer even death for a principle. In a world of want and violence, a religion that was pure and humble and preaching a message of hope (the promise of a blessed life after death) was embraced with enthusiasm.

Pachomian monasteries
In Upper Egypt, near Akhmim, there was a hermitage where Palomen was spiritual leader. Under him, St Pachom, one of the great pillars of the Coptic Church (c.AD 290–346), received initiation. St Pachom saw the advantages of linking together the different communities and founding monasteries. He introduced the 'cenobitic' way of life (derived from the Greek 'common' and 'life'). He was so highly regarded that by the time he died, some thirty years after receiving initiation, there were more than eleven Pachomian monasteries in Upper Egypt, including two for women.

Cenobitic life, which greatly influenced the monastic movement throughout the Mediterranean world, was a combination of asceticism with communal living. Daily activity was organised by vigorously enforced rules regarding clothing, food, work, hours of worship and sleep. Land was brought back to productivity and social and economic life was re-established. Pachom's contribution to Christianity is recognised by the Vatican, where his birthday is commemorated.

Christianity became a protected religion in the time of Constantine the Great and it was officially recognised as the faith of the Roman Empire, and hence of Egypt, in the reign of Theodosius (AD 379–395). The National Church of Egypt, however, was only established in AD 451 when, at the Council of Chalcedon, Egypt separated from the Eastern church. This was due to the controversy, which had developed over a century before, on interpretations of doctrine, especially on the nature of Christ.

Thenceforth the Copts recognised their own Pope and Patriarch at Alexandria, and followed the teachings of St Mark. The Coptic calendar begins its era on 29 August, AD 284, the 'Era of the Martyrs'. commemorating those who died for their faith in the reign of Diocletian.

The name Copt is a corruption of the Greek *Aigyptos*, which is derived from the ancient Egyptian name for Memphis: '*Hikaptah*' or 'House of the Spirit of Ptah'. The Coptic language is the Egyptian vernacular written in the Greek alphabet with the addition of seven extra characters derived from demotic, the last stage of hieroglyphics; it continued to be used until the 13th century, when it was eclipsed by Arabic. It has, however, survived in the Church liturgy and in some vernacular Arabic names, especially in the names of the Coptic months and their divisions into 'tens' of days, which are derived from the names of ancient Egyptian gods. For example, the month of *Tut* is derived from Thoth, and *Hatûr* from Hathor.

Coptic Art and Architecture

During the early Christian period, artistic inspiration was drawn from two sources; Graeco-Roman and indigenous. Unfortunately, few Christian structures survived destruction during the Diocletian era. One can best see the persistence of Greek influence, however, in architectural features such as the niche and in artistic motifs such as the fish.

The question of the persistence of ancient symbolism in Christian art remains controversial. There is little doubt, however, that Gnostic literature and ancient tradition prompted artistic invention.

It must be remembered that the bulk of the population could not read. Through the medium of familiar imagery new religious ideas were promoted.

The archangel Michael weighing souls in the balance is akin to the ancient Egyptian god of wisdom, Thoth, weighing the heart of the deceased in the scales of justice (page 167). St George on horseback crushing evil beneath his horse's hooves, recalls to mind Horus striking down Set, the incarnation of wickedness (page 14). It has not passed unnoticed by scholars that the Spirit or Holy Ghost in the early Church descended in the form of winged dove like the ancient *Ba* (page 87).

Seigfried Morenz, the German scholar, suggests that the life of Joseph the Carpenter depicted on a fifth-century Coptic manuscript gives details of his death that closely resemble those of Osiris: Jesus sits at his head and Mary at his feet, much as Horus stood at the head of Osiris and Isis at his feet in the Egyptian myth.

During the fourth and fifth centuries, the monastic way of life was spreading and churches were built in great number. There was a radical break with the past, especially as regards burial customs. Some of the bishops and patriarchs, on their demise, were clothed in the robes they had worn for religious services. These textiles, which had become known as Coptic tapestries, have been found in vast quantities in the graveyards in the Fayoum and in Upper Egypt, especially around Assiut and Akhmim. The earliest such fabrics were woven on a purple background, in the traditional technique inherited from the ancient Egyptians. The themes were nymphs, garlands, the cross, the fish and the hare, with geometric designs.

At first all the weaving was on linen. Only later was wool used, by which time vine and grape themes had become popular. Animals were woven among branches, biting the fruit of the trees. Peacocks, parrots and ducks were popular themes, as well as some half-animal, half-bird creatures. These Coptic textiles developed into one of the finest of all the minor Coptic arts, showing a great sense of liveliness in the stylized figures.

The costly art of mummification was falling into disuse. The bodies of ordinary people were wrapped in their clothing and interred as quickly as possible. Over the graves, however, tombstones were raised that were shaped like the ancient stelae. They bore the name, date of birth and death of the deceased, and many echoed the petitions and supplications inscribed in hieroglyphics on the tombs of the ancient Egyptians. The rounded top of many an early tombstone was decorated with the drooping wings of the protective vulture-goddess Nekhbet.

From the end of the fifth century, Coptic tradition reached its full maturity. Some of the monasteries in Upper Egypt were to have widespread influence on Christian architecture; among these are the White Monastery and the Red Monastery near Sohag and the Monastery of St Simeon at Aswan. These pre-Islamic Christian structures in the Nile valley indicate many features of the indigenous tradition.

Monasteries, which necessarily had to be at the site of a natural well or spring, were fortresses; the outer walls were usually massive and undecorated; some bear a striking resemblance, from a distance, to an Egyptian temple. Within the monastery were one or more churches. The earliest churches had simple ground plans in three main divisions: the atrium, the nave and the semi-circular apse.

The atrium was a forecourt, surrounded by a colonnade (colonnaded cloister). To the rear was a porch, the narthex, preceded by stairs, much like the terrace to the rear of the open court of a temple. The porch gave access to the main body of the church through doorways (usually of wood), whose number was dictated by the number of aisles. The double-colonnaded nave, like that of a hypostyle hall, had side aisles, and usually terminated in another porch, or transept, which spread the width of the church. There was a formal separation of the main body of the church from the inner chambers, where only those in holy orders could pass. This separation was by means of a rail or screen, often inlaid. Beyond lay the semi-circular apse.

In the White Monastery (Sohag) and in the Monastery of St Simeon (Aswan), there are two additional semi-circular apses, one on each side of the central apse, facing each other. Thus did the traditional sanctuaries to the three gods of an ancient triad correspond, in a church, to three apses. The central apse held the altar to the saint; it had a canopy that was often supported on pillars. The two side apses were for use either on the saint's feast day or for some religious celebration, it being a canon of Coptic law that neither the altar nor the vessels and vestments may be used twice on the same day.

The earliest Christian churches were not designed by professional architects. A monk or a priest drew up the plan and ordered the decoration, drawing naturally from indigenous sources. At Abydos, for example, where the temple of Seti I is uniquely dedicated to seven deities (page 22), the church in the **Monastery of St Moses** (also known as the Monastery of St Dimiana) has seven rectangular sanctuaries (*haikals*), and above each of the seven doorways are icons of the respective patron saints to whom they are dedicated: St Anthony, the Holy Virgin, St Moses, St Michael, St Dimiana, St George and St John the Baptist.

The soft sandstone used in Upper Egypt was particularly adaptable to architectural ornamentation. The sculptured friezes show sharp, deeply cut and distinct stone working, especially on the capitals of the columns, which became more and more stylized. Vines and acanthus were popular decorative motifs; the latter was slowly replaced by palm fronds or vine leaves, sometimes with the cross included in the leaf motif. The artists who had a taste for geometric forms, as is clear from their arabesques, were extremely adept at wood carving. The altars, doors and screens are among the oldest and finest wood carvings of the Coptic era.

A wealth of utilitarian objects were left at the monastic centres: bronze vases, bowls, candelabra, lamps, clay stands for clay pitchers and pottery of various kinds. In Upper Egypt the frog-shaped lamp was popular. Churches were decorated with ceramics and glassware (lamps and phials). Ostrich eggs, considered the symbol of the resurrection, were sometimes suspended in front of the screen. Above the screen separating the nave from the inner chambers was usually a row of icons.

Mural decoration only started in the fourth century. These were painted on the stuccoed walls of a church and in the niches. The scenes were from the lives of the apostles and the saints, or the miracles they performed. Many an ancient temple was converted into a church; the reliefs of the ancient gods were plastered over, and Christian themes were painted. Sometimes an apse was built from inscribed stones that had fallen from ancient temples. Columns from Graeco-Roman structures were used for the nave and aisles. The *Ankh* or Key of Life was sometimes chiselled into the form of a cross.

The artists painted in pure bold colours, never in half-tones. All the figures were shown in frontal position and always with serene smiling faces. There were no scenes of torture, of terror or of hell. Christ was painted enthroned and surrounded by angels, or shown blessing a figure beside Him – Christ the King and never the suffering servant. The Virgin Mother and Child were a frequently painted theme. Sometimes a row of venerated anchorites, monks and the founders of monsteries were depicted.

In watching the mystery play of The Nativity, the Egyptians recognised in the Holy Virgin and Child their own beloved Isis and

Horus; Isis, too, had guarded her son from those who wished them evil. The story of Jesus healing a blind man reminded them of Thoth, who spat on the wound in Horus' eye (lost during one of his battles with Set), in order to heal it. The suffering and crucifixion of Christ and His resurrection, recalled to mind their own just and beloved ancestor, Osiris, who was slain and yet lived again.

The rite of baptism or purification with water had its origins in the distant past, as well as the vapour of incense that was used to create a sympathetic atmosphere for drawing man and God together. The Egyptians readily embraced a religion that gave them familiar altars and priesthoods and 'messengers' from heaven. They knew well that 'the sanctuary of God abhorreth noisy demonstrations' and that they should 'chant not God's offices too loudly', because the ancient wisdoms of the sage Kagemni had survived in tradition.

Perhaps it was easier for the Nile valley dwellers to understand the Trinity than many other early Christians, in view of their own triads (triple deities in one temple or threefold names representing different aspects of the same personality under which an ancient god was addressed). The doctrine of future rewards and punishments seemed no different to the day of judgement for both good and wicked in the Court of Osiris, when charity, honesty, justice and virtue were the keys to a life everlasting. The Egyptians had long seen their dead as 'the imperishable ones' in heaven. And the concept of hell with thirst, fire, demons and spirits was startlingly familiar from 'The sun's journey in the Underworld' (page 96).

The Egyptians preferred to have an actual object of religious identification as a focal point of worship rather than abstract dogma. In many villages the people claimed that a relic, or relics, of a saint or martyr had been found. They started to build shrines to house them. This practice – which is reminiscent of the provinces (nomes) of ancient Egypt each claiming possession of a part of the body of Osiris and erecting shrines in his honour (page 19) – had become so widespread that St Shenuda, Abbot of the White Monastery near Sohag, early in the fifth century, severely criticised the villagers in Upper Egypt. St Shenuda tried to purge Christian teachings and society from all traces of Graeco-Roman and Byzantine influence, destroy heretical literature and purge Christianity of 'every kind of magic'; a phrase that appears frequently in the Nag Hammadi Library.

In view of their age-old tradition one cannot help but wonder whether a celebrant priest in Upper Egypt intoned the liturgy 'Amon...' and not 'Amen' at the end of a prayer.

DESCRIPTION

Christian monuments have been embellished, enlarged and rebuilt by successive generations. Descriptions are given only to those structures that date to the pre-Islamic period, and the highly selective choice is based on the following:

Monastery Deir el Muharraq, south-west of Assiut (below)	This is the only monastery in Upper Egypt that is still inhabited by monks (the other inhabited monasteries are at Wadi Natrun and on the Red Sea coast). There are scores of other monasteries in Upper Egypt, especially around Esna, which are now used for Sunday services only.
The White Monastery and the **Red Monastery** near Sohag (page 208)	These are two of the most well-known of the eleven Pachomian monasteries in Upper Egypt
Basilica at Dendera (page 209)	This is one of the earliest structures of the Christian era.
Christian structures at Luxor (page 209)	The Theban area is studded with monasteries; hermits and monks who could not afford to build monasteries, however, used ancient tombs and temples. Some of these are identified.
Monastery of St Simeon, south-west of Aswan (page 211)	This is the most famous monastery in Upper Egypt and one of the most beautiful.

The Monastery of Deir el Muharraq

This monastery is situated about sixty-five kilometres south-west of Assiut and is best approached from al Qusia. It is the largest monastery in Upper Egypt, long known for its charitable work among the villagers. Unlike many desert monasteries that are totally isolated, Deir el Muharraq is located at the edge of the agricultural land; the monastery buildings are contained within a surrounding wall of irregular shape.

Deir el Muharraq belongs to the group of monasteries founded by St Pachom (*Aba Bakhum* in Arabic) and his successors. Its history is not clear. According to tradition, the Church of the Blessed Virgin was the first church to be built in Egypt (the monks claim that it was constructed after St Mark's arrival in Egypt about AD 60). It was built on the site of a cave where the Holy Family is said to have stayed for three years. Biblical scholars and historians agree that it was in a cave at Deir el Muharraq that Joseph dreamed that an angel of the Lord appeared, informing him of Herod's death and bidding him to take Jesus and Mary and return to Palestine.

The Church of the Blessed Virgin is situated more than a metre below the level of the court. The altar stone, which bears the date 11 December, 747, is shaped like a stele. St Peter and St Paul built another church above the original one, only part of which remains. It was demolished in the nineteenth century, when the new Church of St George was built on the site.

The White Monastery near Sohag

This Monastery, dedicated to St Shenuda, dates from the fourth century. It is approached from the southern part of the riverine village of Sohag, about $4\frac{1}{2}$ kilometres westwards. It bears a strong resemblance, from a distance, to an Egyptian temple. Neither this monastery nor the Red Monastery have resident monks. Together they formed the largest community of monks in Upper Egypt during the fifth century.

The Church of St Shenuda occupies the largest part of the monastery, and it clearly shows architectural features that were inspired by indigenous tradition: the three semi-circular apses and surrounding chambers and the separation of these inner chambers from the nave and narthex (terrace). The latter, which is preceded by stairs, leads to galleries.

The three apses are dedicated to St Shenuda at the centre, to St George and the Virgin Mary on each side. They are vaulted and made of burnt-brick. The walls are decorated with columns, each surmounted by architraves forming niches. The deeply cut stone-work is characteristic of the period.

The library of this monastery contained letters that represent one of the original and chief sources of Coptic literature.

The Red Monastery near Sohag

This monastery, which is smaller than the White Monastery, is situated about three kilometres north of it. The Red Monastery was also built at the edge of the cultivated land; in fact, it is in the midst of the village.

The Church of St Bishoi has many features similar to the Church of St Shenuda: the three-aisled nave with gallery and the unusual

The Basilica beside the Temple of Dendera

freestanding columns; these columns frame niches that are hollowed out in the semi-circular apses.

Both the White and Red Monasteries are characterised by great simplicity and have massive outer walls with no decoration.

The Basilica at Dendera

The ruins of this basilica are situated near the Birth-House of the temple of Hathor. It is built of sandstone. Some of the blocks from the Birth House were reused in its construction.

This is one of the earliest Roman basilicas with a wide central aisle or nave, and two side aisles preceded by a narthex on the west, with lateral semi-circular apses at the end. It is large and roomy with decorated recesses.

It is possible that this church marked the famous Christian centre of the fourth century for it was stated by St Jerome that somewhere in the neighbourhood of Dendera fifty thousand monks assembled to celebrate the Easter festival.

Christian Structures at Luxor

Literally thousands of anchorites lived in the ancient tombs at Luxor, especially the nobles' tombs on the hillside of Sheikh el Kurna. Some, however, occupied tombs in the Valley of the Kings.

210

The tomb of Ramses IV (No. 2) was occupied by early Christians, who inscribed Coptic graffiti on the walls.

During the fourth century hermitages spread, and Luxor became famous for its monastic settlements. Thus, there was a mixture of solitaries on the one hand, and Pachomian-type cenobitic communities on the other.

Many of the great temples were converted into monastic centres. Around the Mortuary Temple of Ramses III at Medinet Habu, a large Christian community flourished. Some lived inside the ancient temple where the second court was converted into a church. The remains of this church were only cleared in 1895. A library was found at Medinet Habu with records written on papyrus and pottery sherds (ostraka).

The Graeco-Roman Temple of Deir el Medina (page 167) owes its name to the Christian monastery into which it was converted; some of the inscriptions in this nearly perfectly preserved temple were mutilated by the early Christians. The Festival Temple of Thutmose III at Karnak (page 68) was also converted into a church, as well as the Court of Amenhotep III in the Luxor temple (page 58).

In some temples we owe the preservation of the ancient reliefs to the early Christians; they covered the 'heathen' reliefs with plaster and thus protected them.

The Monastery of St Simeon in its desert setting

Interior of the Monastery of St Simeon

The Monastery of St Simeon at Aswan

This is one of the largest and most well preserved of the monasteries; it is dedicated to a local saint who lived there in the fifth century. It is built on a hill in the western desert about one and half kilometres from the southern tip of Elephantine.

Of its origins we know little, though it is believed to date from very early times. The present construction dates from the seventh century. There is evidence of restoration in the tenth century, and the monastery was abandoned in the thirteenth century; the reason may have been lack of water or constant attack from roving bands of nomads.

The surrounding wall is over six metres high; the upper part is sun-dried brick and the lower is rough hewn stone sunk in the rock. At intervals along the enclosure wall there are towers. These have raised the possibility that the monks may have chosen a deserted and ruined Roman fortress in which to construct their monastery.

The low face of the cliff divides the monastery into an upper and a lower level from north to south. The entrance to the east leads to the lower level, which comprises a vaulted central corridor; on the eastern wall is a painting of Christ enthroned with the archangel Michael and six apostles by His side. The small chambers on each side contained from six to eight beds for the monks. The upper level, approached by a staircase in the southern angle, is similarly arranged; monks lived in cells opening out on each side of the corridor. Below the main building are some rock-hewn cells and a rock-chapel that is painted with saints.

At the northern end of the upper level is the main building, which itself is double-storied. The church lies to the south-east, between the building itself and the outer wall. The roof was originally a series of domes supported by square pillars. The domed apse at the east has a well-preserved painting of enthroned Christ, His hand raised in benediction. He is flanked by angels, two on each side. The two main angels have wings, long hair and splendid robes. On either side of the recesses are seven seated figures. Around the walls are paintings of Saints Michael, George and the archangel Gabriel with the Twelve Apostles. A cave leading off the north-west corner of the chapel is believed to have been the dwelling place of the patron saint. It has painted walls and decorative ceiling.

The northern wall of the upper level of the monastery is actually built over the enclosure wall. The windows look out over the steep cliff. The desert slopes towards the Nile valley. This is one of the most picturesque of Egypt's desert scenes and gives a sense of the mystic appeal of the desolate wilderness.

CONCLUSION: CHANGE AND CONTINUITY

Many thousands of years have passed since man first settled in *Kmt*, the Black Land: Egypt. The country has known great periods of growth and development, and others of decline and decadence; it has experienced cultural, political, economic and spiritual growth, and it has known, too, subjugation, humiliation and corruption in one form or another.

Time and again Egypt has been exposed to elements that stimulated its development, aggravated a warlike spirit, changed its outlook, inspired styles of clothing, and even changed opinions of the desirable attributes of the female figure – the fleshier body of the Graeco-Roman period rather than the slim look of the Old Kingdom.

Yet, alongside the differences between Pharaonic, Graeco-Roman and early Christian periods, we have here traced a tradition that manifested itself in art – through familiar imagery – in architecture, and in such crafts as weaving. There are, in addition, fundamental resemblances that stand out less vividly but which show a remarkable continuity: in location, tradition, ritual and ideology.

There are places in Egypt that are regarded as holy, which have a long history of sanctity. Many of the ancient monuments, as we have shown, were transformed into Christian churches. Mosques have, in turn, been constructed on the sites of former Christian chapels. In the Luxor temple, for example, the area lying between the Hypostyle Hall and the Sanctuary was converted into a shrine (page 58), and the mosque of Abu el Hagag was built in the court of Ramses II in the same temple (page 57).

Tradition persists in numerous festivals. One of these is the Muslim '*moulid*' that is celebrated during the month of *Shaaban* in Luxor, which closely resembles the ancient Egyptian *Opet* festival pages 57–8); sheikhs emerge from the mosque bearing sailing boats that they place on carriages; these traverse a city that is bedecked with flags and filled with rejoicing people. The Feast of St George, which is celebrated by both Copts and Muslims at Mit Damsis, near Mansoura in the Delta, is another example; it closely resembles the Festival of Bastet described by Herodotus as a wine-drinking boat-festival with dancing and fanfare. And '*Shem el Nessim*' ('Smell the Breeze'), Egypt's most popular festival, which is celebrated on the first day of spring, undoubtedly had its origins in the country's ancient past, since it is not observed in any other country. The people wake up at dawn and picnic outdoors on spring onions, *feseekh* (salted fish) and *foul* (beans).

Apart from religious belief in the concept of the soul, an afterlife, resurrection and judgement, religious ritual provides the most clear examples of continuity: sacrificing animals, use of incense, purification with water, pilgrimages to the graves of the deceased with flowers (and sometimes food and drink) and casting sand on the head as a sign of bereavement. Also, the Egyptians are still a deeply superstitious people. Written charms or amulets are used to safeguard health, grant fertility and protect against evil – especially the Evil Eye (the belief that to look with envy causes grave consequences).

Change and continuity is not as paradoxical as it sounds. For although there are very real political, social and ideological differences between the Pharaonic, Graeco-Roman and early Christian periods, there is also a static factor. Egyptian leadership, for example, has always been associated with that great source of life: the Nile. Through progressive civilizations efforts have been made to harness its waters. From the earliest pharaohs who ceremoniously wielded pickaxes to open new canals, to the present day, when the river has been harnessed by the High Dam, leaders – ancient Egyptians, Greeks, Romans, Mameluks, Kings and Presidents – have built canals, barrages, aqueducts and dams. Faith in a leader who is provider, protector and controller of water is, therefore, a factor that has outlived change.

In rural Egypt, where family ties are strongest, and technological advances are least felt, there is also least change. The famer tends his land with his wooden plough, transports produce on his faithful donkey, and draws water by such ancient devices as the waterwheel driven by patient buffaloes, as did his forebears. Soilbound and conservative, the Egyptian farmer preceded even Egypt's first period of great development, and he has outlived the rise and fall of many others. His life is adjusted to the pace of the crop and the predictable rhythm of the seasons. He seeks no change, because the means of continuity reposes in the black soil beneath his feet.

SUGGESTIONS FOR FURTHER READING

ADAMS, WILLIAM Y. *Nubia, Corridor to Africa*, Allen Lane, London, 1977

BREASTED, JAMES, *A History of Egypt*, Hodder & Stoughton, London, 1950

CLAYTON, PETER A. *The Rediscovery of Ancient Egypt: Artists and Travellers in the 19th Century*, Thames and Hudson, London 1982

FRANKFORT, H. *Ancient Egyptian Religion; an interpretation*, Harper, New York, 1961

GARDINER, SIR ALAN, *Egypt of the Pharaohs*, Oxford University Press, 1961

HABACHI, LABIB, *The Obelisks of Egypt*. Charles Scribner's Sons, New York, and J. M. Dent, London, 1978

KAMIL, JILL. *Luxor; a Guide to Ancient Thebes*, Longman, London and New York, 3rd ed. 1982

Sakkara; a Guide to the Necropolis and the site of Memphis, Longman, London and New York, 1978

The Ancient Egyptians; How they Lived and Worked. David and Charles, Newton Abbot, 1976

KEES, H. *Ancient Egypt; a Cultural Topography*. Faber & Faber, London, 1961

KEATING, R. *Nubian Rescue*, Robert Hale, London and Hawthorn Books, New York, 1975

MEINARDUS, OTTO. *Christian Egypt; Ancient and Modern*, American University in Cairo Press, Cairo 1978

MURNANE, WILLIAM J. *United with Eternity; a Concise Guide to the Monuments of Medinet Habu*. American University in Cairo Press, Cairo 1979

NIMS, CHARLES F. *Thebes of the Pharaohs* Elek Books, London, 1965

TRIGGER, BRUCE G. *Nugia under the Pharaohs*, Thames and Hudson, London, 1976

WEEKS, KENT, *et al.*, *Egyptology and the Social Sciences*, American University in Cairo Press, Cairo 1979

WILSON, JOHN A. *The Culture of Egypt*. University of Chicago Press, 1956

INDEX

Note: Italicised figures refer to illustrations on page cited. References to maps and plans are so described.

226